FROM PANIC
TO PEACE OF MIND:

Overcoming Panic and Agoraphobia

C.B. SCRIGNAR, M.S., M.D.
Clinical Professor of Psychiatry
Tulane University School of Medicine
Adjunct Professor
Tulane University School of Social Work
New Orleans

ILLUSTRATED BY ARTHUR NEAD

BRUNO PRESS — NEW ORLEANS, LOUISIANA

Published by Bruno Press
A Division of BTC, Inc.
2627 General Pershing Street, New Orleans, LA 70115

NOTE: All medications mentioned in this book are consistent with standards set by the United States Food and Drug Administration and the general medical community. As medical research and practice advance, however, therapy standards may change. For this reason the author recommends that readers follow the advice of a physician directly involved in their care or the care of a family member.

Library of Congress Cataloging in Publication Data

Scrignar, C.B. (Chester B.)
From Panic to Peace of Mind: Overcoming Panic and Agoraphobia

    p. cm.
Bibliography: p. Includes index

1. Panic disorders — Treatment.
2. Agoraphobia — Treatment

I. Title.
    [DNLM: 1. Agoraphobia. 2. Panic.   WM 178S434f]

RC535. S38 1991   616.85'22306 — dc20   91–1358
DNLM/DCL

ISBN 0-945032-02-1

Last digit is print number: 9 8 7 6 5 4 3 2 1

Printed in the United States of America on acid-free paper

TO DORIS, DIANA AND ALBERT

Preface

Anxiety is the most wide spread emotional disorder in the United States and probably the world. Millions of people suffer from panic attacks (panic disorder), an inability to leave home unaccompanied (agoraphobia), excessive worry (generalized anxiety disorder), the debilitating effect of obsessions and compulsive rituals (obsessive compulsive disorder), irrational fear of objects or social situations (simple or social phobia), or a persistent emotional reaction following trauma (post-traumatic stress disorder). Anxiety disorders can interfere with almost every area of behavior including relationships with family and friends, performance at work, and the simple enjoyment of life. Alcoholism, drug abuse, psychosomatic illness, and depression can also result from chronic anxiety.

No one is immune from the effects of anxiety. The night before *The Beagle* was to sail, Charles Darwin experienced a panic attack, almost cancelling his epic-making voyage which led to the theory of evolution. Untreated panic attacks can disrupt the voyage of life for many panic prone patients. Phobias and fears complicate the lives of anxious people as they struggle with daily existence. The mental habit of worrying causes anxiety leading to a number of physiologic symptoms and unnecessary visits to doctors. Whereas normal anxiety alerts an individual to potential danger, pathologic anxiety only serves to perpetuate unwarranted fear. Thus many combat veterans and civilians exposed to traumatic events suffer needlessly from chronic anxiety. Some obsessive compulsive individuals constantly wash their hands and engage in cleaning rituals as they attempt to rid themselves of imaginary germs.

Although theories related to the "fight or flight response" developed by Walter Canon and the "general adaptation syndrome" by Hans Selye have shed light on anxiety, stress, and survival, it has been only in recent times that panic disorder and agoraphobia were correctly correlated. In 1980 for the first time, panic disorder was included in the *Diagnostic and Statistical Manual of Mental Disorders* by the American Psychiatric Association. In the past decade, research has led to a better understanding and more effective treatment of panic disorder, agoraphobia, and the other anxiety disorders.

This book describes the anxiety disorders and highlights the signs, symptoms, and current treatment of panic and agoraphobia. Panic disorder is a perplexing mental syndrome because the symptoms appear to indicate a physical illness. Panic disorder with agoraphobia adds more confusion due to the fact that the phobia is often disguised within the fabric of panic. Hence, patients and sometimes clinicians fail to appreciate that agoraphobia is a consequence of panic and both are mental disorders.

In the behavioral sciences, the conceptualization of anxiety takes into account biological, cognitive-behavioral, and psychosocial factors. The biological component consists of the complex activity of the brain and treatment usually involves medication. Thinking, learning, and conditioning form the basis of a cognitive-behavioral approach to anxiety, while treatment consists of cognitive restructuring, exposure treatment (systematic desensitization), and relaxation training. The psychosocial component of anxiety focuses on the environment and its impact on an individual. When considering the cause and the cure of anxiety disorders, one must analyze all three of these constituents.

In another book, *Stress Strategies: The Treatment of the Anxiety Disorders*, I attempted to simplify the biologic, behavioral, and psychosocial framework for anxiety under the heading "The Three E's". This schema involves the environment (one's surroundings), encephalic activity (thoughts and visual images of the mind), and endogenous events (biological and physiological sensations of the brain and body). I have included the concept of the Three E's in this book to help the reader understand, not only the cause of anxiety, but also the rationale for treatment. Accordingly, when the environment produces stress and anxiety, changes in surroundings can reverse the process. Likewise, reliving unpleasant memories from the past, worrying excessively, or anticipating anxiety (encephalic activities) can be reduced by certain thought control techniques. Excessive brain activity (endogenous sensations), can be controlled by specific medications. Also, when the mind and body are on edge, relaxation treatment helps lower mental and physical tension. Other antianxiety interventions which impact on the Three E's include: education-enhanced communication, involvement of the spouse or significant other, good nutrition, daily exercise, and the elimination of stress from work. Pleasure counteracts anxiety so that increasing social and recreational activities help to dispel the crippling aspects of anxiety.

Self-directed treatment and the utilization of a support group may be all that is necessary to achieve good results. A professional is not absolutely necessary unless medication is required. Professionals need not be neglected; they can be used as consultants or therapists if obstacles to successful treatment arise. After the treatment plan is implemented, motivation to change and persistence are the two most important characteristics associated with a successful outcome.

C. B. Scrignar, M.D.
New Orleans, Louisiana

Aknowledgements

Many people contribute directly or indirectly to a book as it is being written. I would like to thank all of my colleagues, friends, and patients who helped mold my ideas into the final form of this book. My special thanks to Michael Duffy who read every draft of the manuscript; his ideas and suggestions have greatly improved the quality of the book. Dr. Daniel Winstead, chairman of the department of psychiatry at Tulane University School of Medicine and Dr. David Mielke, chief of psychiatry at the Veterans Administration Hospital in New Orleans were extremely helpful during the early organization of the book. Drs. Ray Swan and Doug Greve, good friends, fishing buddies, and colleagues for many, many years, critiqued early drafts of the manuscript and helped guide the book to its completion. My deep appreciation and gratitude goes to Drs. Ralph Slovenko and James Knight, both friends of long duration, for their wisdom and wonderful comments. Harriet Hanshaw, Vernon Crawford and Deborah Moncrief gave freely of their time during the organization of the book and came up with ideas for illustrations. I wish to thank Arthur Nead for his talent in translating ideas into art. Muldrow Etheredge, who has the unique qualifications of both lawyer and social worker, lent his support during many discussions as the book progressed to its completion. I wish to express my thanks to John and Lorraine Hamwey of ABC Publications Inc., Westwood, Massachusetts, for their energy and work in the design and printing of *From Panic to Peace of Mind*. Both John and Lorraine have enhanced the quality of the book and I am deeply grateful.

Finally, a double thanks goes to my wife, Mary for her invaluable assistance from the first draft to the last. Mary has shared the tedium associated with editorial tasks. Only a loving wife would endure the social deprivation associated with the writing of a book. Love and kisses to you Mary.

Contents

Part I

Panic Disorder

Pan, The God of Panic

1

Scared To Death

Imagine walking through a forest and seeing a vague form which appears to be half beast and half man. Curiosity impels you to make a closer inspection and if you are brave and adventuresome, you stealthily creep forward for a better look. You see a dwarfish creature with the legs and tail of a goat. The upper half of the body looks like a man, but the horns and ears are goat-like. The man/beast has a bearded face and is playing an eerie tune with a flute-like instrument. You are mesmerized by the sight and sound of the spectacle. The reedy notes stop abruptly and the creature, aware of your presence, turns slowly and stares at you. As the stare turns to menace, you realize that you have encroached upon the territory of Pan, the god of fields, forests, wild animals, flocks, and shepherds. As Pan approaches, do you feel scared to death; do you experience a *Pan*ic attack?

Almost everyone has had a panic attack during their lifetime. I had a panic attack years ago when I was a young instructor of psychiatry at Tulane University. I was showing the chairman of the department around a large community center which I was proposing for use in a juvenile delinquency project. At the end of the tour, I was not feeling well. My chairman asked me what was wrong, and I replied that I really didn't know. In an alarming manner, he told me to lie down on the floor and put my legs on a chair. He took my pulse and found that it was quite fast. He then called the medical school for an internist and an ambulance. A doctor arrived, took my blood pressure, listened to my heart, and told me that there was probably nothing wrong with me. Nevertheless, I was taken to a hospital in an ambulance for an examination. At the hospital, the internist informed me that the physical examination and electrocardiogram were normal. I told him that I had had a gastrointestinal disturbance for the past two days. He replied that a virus was probably responsible for my symptoms. I was discharged from the hospital the following day.

During the next few months, I noticed that whenever I was fatigued from overwork or overplay and became overheated for any reason, my heart raced, the palms of my hands became moist, and I felt very anxious. Each time this happened frightening thoughts went through my mind, "What's wrong with me? I'm going to faint. I feel panicky." An analysis of the events which I had experienced at the community center led me to the following explanation. I contracted a virus which affected my gastrointestinal tract. This created a disruption of my normal bodily functions and resulted in a feeling of malaise. Walking through the unairconditioned environment of the community center during a hot and humid summer day intensified this feeling of discomfort. My chairman, witnessing my distress, assumed that I was having a heart attack. He was a man that I respected, so I complied with his request to lie on the floor and put my legs in an elevated position. In alarm I thought to myself, "My God, he thinks I'm having a heart attack! *Am* I having a heart attack?" Almost immediately, I could feel adrenalin pumping into my body, followed by a rapidly beating heart, accelerated breathing, and a feeling of dizziness and panic. I said to myself, "There is something going on in my body, and I feel awful." These thoughts and feelings disappeared as I relaxed after a complete examination in the hospital. At the time of my discharge, I was over the virus, I felt fine, and I returned to work. A few weeks later I became aware of anxiety symptoms when I was tired and hot. The feeling of fatigue, combined with the heat, triggered my nervous system. This was intensified by the self-statements: "What's wrong with me? Am I having another attack?" When I made a correct analysis of the situation, my thinking changed. Then I used some techniques of muscle relaxation to decrease anxiety. After employing these methods repeatedly, mastery over my anxiety symptoms was achieved and I was relieved of my panic.

ARE PANIC ATTACKS COMMON?

People who have periodic panic attacks think that they are "oddballs" and the only ones in the world with panic and anxiety symptoms. Statistics belie this belief. A recent survey conducted by the National Institute of Mental Health (NIMH) revealed that anxiety is the most widespread mental disorder in the United States, affecting 8.3 percent or 13.1 million Americans over the age of 18. Anxiety disorders are more chronic, persistent, and recurrent than previously thought. It has been reported that 10 to 15 percent of the population is predisposed to a greater risk for anxiety disorders and this vulnerability may be sustained throughout the life cycle. Almost 10 percent of the people surveyed by NIMH answered *yes* to the question: "Have you ever had a spell when all of a sudden you felt frightened, anxious, or very tense in situations when most people wouldn't be afraid?" Dr. James C. Ballenger said at the eighth annual meeting of the Phobia Society of America that fully 30 to 40 percent of Americans have at least one panic attack each year. About 17 percent suffer two to four attacks, and four to six percent had at least one panic attack each week for three consecutive weeks. Mental health professionals have become more aware of the diagnosis and treatment of this anxiety disorder, so today there is little reason why most patients with panic disorder cannot be successfully treated.

HISTORY OF PANIC DISORDER

Fruitful research that led to the diagnosis of panic disorder began about 30 years ago. In 1959, Dr. Donald F. Klein started investigating the effects of a medication (the antidepressant, imipramine) upon hospitalized psychiatric patients. At the time, Dr. Klein and his associates were studying patients who incorrectly received the diagnosis of schizophrenia. Symptomatically, the subjects were highly anxious patients with periodic panic attacks and marked social impairment. After receiving imipramine, these chronically anxious patients no longer had panic attacks. At first, because the patients were not properly diagnosed, these results were confusing. A reexamination, however, revealed that these chronically anxious patients were not suffering from schizophrenia but from panic disorder with agoraphobia. This important discovery led the way to a new classification for panic attacks. In 1980, the American Psychiatric Association first included panic disorder in its Diagnostic and Statistical Manual of Mental Disorders (DSM), and this official recognition stimulated much activity in basic research and the development of effective treatment.

WHAT CAUSES A PANIC ATTACK?

No one knows precisely what causes panic attacks. Most researchers believe that environmental influences and heredity combine to make a person vulnerable to a panic attack. Panic is a mental disorder characterized by certain signs and symptoms and a well defined clinical course. Typically, panic disorder begins in early adulthood, with the onset occurring between the ages of 18 and 35 (average age 26). Occasionally, attacks in the early teens or even as late as the fifth decade have been reported. Panic disorder is equally distributed between the sexes, while panic with agoraphobia is twice as prevalent in females.

Both biological and psychological factors appear to predispose individuals to panic disorder. Various studies have established that a risk of 25 to 32 percent is present in first-degree relatives of panic disorder patients, suggesting a genetic transmission. Other studies have shown that generalized anxiety and physical symptoms preceded the diagnosis of panic disorder. Psychological predisposing factors such as a severe illness, death of a loved one, marital problems, childbirth, or serious problems at work often seem to be related to the onset of a panic attack. However, severe stress does not always precipitate a panic attack. The issue of whether prolonged periods of stress predispose those who develop panic disorder has not been clearly established at this time. It seems reasonable to conclude that individuals who have a genetic predisposition and a nervous system which is overly sensitive to environmental stressors are more likely to develop panic disorder. Once panic disorder has developed, psychological factors play an important role, and psychological interventions are indispensable during treatment.

There are two camps concerning the cause and treatment of panic disorder. Those clinicians favoring a genetic and biological cause of panic disorder advocate the use of medication. Those therapists who lean towards psychological treatment may minimize the importance of medication. Dr. Svenn Torgersen, a noted genetic researcher from Norway, has stated, "There is no evidence that a disorder partly caused by genetic factors is more successfully treated by biochemical therapy than a disorder solely caused by environmental factors. Similarly, psychological therapy does not need to be more effective for a disorder caused by environmental factors than for a disorder strongly influenced by genetics." The simple truth is that at the present time, the best theory to explain panic disorder involves a biological component combined with environmental factors. The best treatment for panic disorder utilizes both biological (medication) and psychological interventions (relaxation, cognitive techniques, exposure treatment, etc.).

THE BRAIN AND PANIC

Basic research is beginning to focus on a location in the brain which is linked to panic disorder. Stimulating certain areas within the brain of animals causes panic. Postoperative studies of humans with gunshot wounds or tumors in the brain also support the idea of a specific anatomic location for panic and anxiety. There is good evidence that the locus coeruleus (the brain's norepinephrine-containing nucleus) plays a central role in the production of panic and anxiety. Acute stress activates the locus coerulrus system (hypothalamus, amygdala, thalamus, cerebral cortex, and the hippocampus). Chemical agents such as caffeine, sodium lactate, yohimbine, and carbon dioxide also activate the locus coeruleus system and can precipitate a panic attack in a majority of patients with panic disorder. Research conducted at the Karolinska Institute in Sweden indicates that the locus coeruleus system responds not only to external stress, but also to internal "threats". Physiological changes such as distension of internal organs, reduction in blood volume or pressure, a thermoregulatory challenge, or hypoglycemia result in activation of the locus coeruleus system. Successful treatment of panic attacks with antipanic medication (Chapter 15) also serves as empirical evidence for a biological component in panic disorder.

Dr. Jerrold F. Rosenbaum, an associate professor of psychiatry at Harvard Medical School, suggests that panic disorder may have an important biological or genetic underpinning (a constitutional predisposition to developing the disorder). Persons prone to panic have a vulnerability to anxiety which emerges later in life and is then, presumably, sustained by a combination of neurophysiological, environmental, and cognitive/psychological factors. Rosenbaum supports his thesis by pointing to studies which indicate an increased risk for anxiety disorders among family members of anxious patients and the high concordance rates observed in identical twins who have developed panic disorder. No doubt a complex interaction of genes, brain physiology and biochemistry, family influences, cultural factors, and learning contribute to the development of panic disorder.

AN UNFORGETTABLE EVENT

Once a person has had a panic attack, the memory of it can last a lifetime. My panic attack occurred over 25 years ago, but I shall never forget it. One panic-stricken patient described an attack in the following way: "Suddenly, without warning, I had this terrible feeling, a feeling of absolute terror. I thought that something really bad was happening to me, but I didn't know what. The feeling was so dreadful that at the time, I thought death would be preferable." Invariably, terrible thoughts race through a victim's mind following an attack. "Will it happen again? Will I die? Will I lose control? Will I go crazy?" Stricken patients begin to forecast panic and develop an outright dread that something bad will happen to them. It is no wonder that most patients with panic disorder have what has been called by Dr. Arthur B. Hardy, "a fear of fear."

ANTICIPATING PANIC AND ANXIETY

Human beings are blessed with the power of abstract thought. The ability to plan ahead and to anticipate future difficulties can be a blessing or a curse. When one begins to anticipate a bad outcome to a future happening, calamitous thoughts stimulate the nervous system and anxiety or fear results. Because a panic attack is an unforgettable and fearful event, panic-prone people begin to worry that it will happen again. Thinking about this possibility generates anxiety. Victims of panic waste many hours on this energy-depleting and self-defeating practice. When panic attacks are frequent, presaging panic and anticipating anxiety are prominent mental mechanisms. Most of the time, anticipation is a fruitless activity that only heightens anxiety. This bad habit (phobic or catastrophic thinking) must be dealt with during treatment.

AVOIDANCE AND PANIC

Avoidance in the face of realistic danger (threat to life or limb) is adaptive and promotes survival. Avoidance in the face of a distasteful or disagreeable environment removes one from an unpleasant situation. Avoidance in the face of a panic attack is understandable as a phobic mechanism which lowers anxiety, but unfortunately, it is irrational and not adaptive. No realistic threat to life or limb exists during a panic attack. Avoiding feared situations and fleeing to a "safe place" is maladaptive because it reinforces phobic behavior. Put another way, a person is rewarded for avoiding situations that are not dangerous in the first place. Coping and confronting irrationally generated anxiety is more adaptive and defeats the phobic reaction of avoidance.

Some patients suffering from panic disorder may have frequent panic attacks and most of the time experience high levels of anxiety. To avoid the uncomfortable feelings of panic and anxiety, victims seek out places where they feel calm and secure. When this behavioral pattern of avoidance becomes pervasive, it is labeled agoraphobia. Fortunately, exposure treatment or systematic desensitization is very effective in overcoming the phobic reaction of agoraphobia (Chapter 16).

UNCONSCIOUS PSYCHOLOGICAL CONFLICTS

Patients with panic disorder frequently ask me, "What is the underlying reason for my panic?" At one time, psychiatrists explored the origin of panic, focusing on developmental issues and unconscious psychological conflicts. Now we know that the symptoms of panic disorder are the problem and do not represent any repressed unconscious conflicts. A close look reveals that the symptoms of panic disorder are intermittent and not constant as would be expected from a continuing psychological conflict. Once proper treatment has been rendered, the symptoms disappear. Symptom substitution does not occur. After treatment, patients resume living in a normal fashion.

THE IMAGINATION AND PANIC

During a panic attack, the internal organs of the body seem to be going "a mile a minute". The commotion inside the body draws the victim's attention to the possibility that something is terribly wrong. As the mind's eye turns inward during a panic attack, the victim monitors bodily sensations for two reasons: first, for a sign or warning of another panic attack, and second, for evidence of symptoms suggesting a serious physical illness. The fear of having a terrible disease becomes a dominant dread. This is especially true when panic attacks are frequent and remain undiagnosed and untreated. Constant somatic complaints and an insistence that something is physically wrong, despite normal results from examinations and a physician's attempts at reassurance, can lead to the labeling of panic-prone patients as hypochondriacs. Physicians who treat the patient's symptoms as inconsequential may have disgruntled patients. The fear of physical illness in the context of a panic disorder must be dealt with before treatment begins.

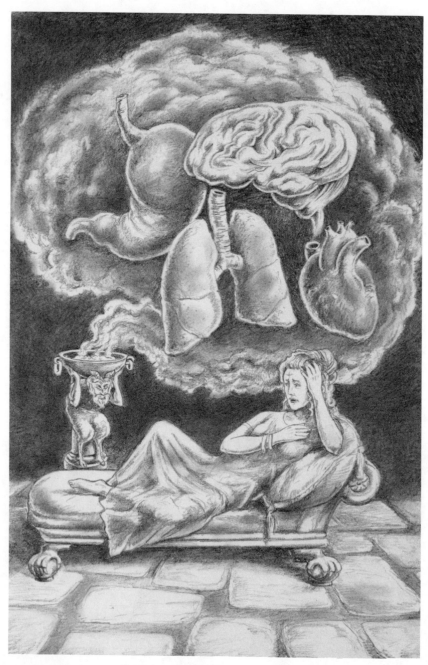

Panic, The Great Pretender

2

Panic — Imagining Physical Illness

Feeling sick, a panic-stricken woman imagines that she has a serious physical illness. Thoughts that she may have heart disease, stomach trouble, lung disease, or a tumor of the brain flood her mind after each panic attack. The distraught woman begins to believe that imagination is equivalent to reality. Panic disorder is the great pretender which mimics physical illness, fooling the victim and sometimes the therapist. Although panic disorder may imitate the signs and symptoms of some physical illness, it is essentially a mental disorder.

PANIC ATTACKS

The American Psychiatric Association defines the essential feature of panic disorder as recurrent and

discrete periods of intense fear or discomfort with at
least four characteristic associated symptoms as listed
in Chart 1. The attacks may occur daily, several times

CHART 1

SYMPTOMS OF PANIC DISORDER*

1. Shortness of breath (dyspnea) or smothering sensations
2. Dizziness, unsteady feelings, or faintness
3. Palpitations or accelerated heart rate (tachycardia)
4. Trembling or shaking
5. Sweating
6. Choking
7. Nausea or abdominal distress
8. Depersonalization or derealization
9. Numbness or tingling sensations (paresthesia)
10. Flushes (hot flashes) or chills
11. Chest pain or discomfort
12. Fear of dying
13. Fear of going crazy or of going out of control

*From: *Diagnostic and Statistical Manual of Mental Disorders* (Third Edition-
Revised). 1987. Washington, D.C. American Psychiatric Association.

Also, often reported by panic disorder patients are the following:

1. Rapid breathing (hyperventilation)
2. Difficulties in swallowing
3. Panic attacks during sleep
4. Intense subjective discomfort (dysphoria)

---

a week, or less frequently, and may persist for a few
minutes or, in rare cases, for hours. Although patients may experience anxiety and physical symptoms
prior to an attack, the sudden onset of fear, terror, or
impending doom is usually a complete surprise. Panic

attacks are typically followed by a period of persistent fear of having another attack. Later in the course of the disturbance, certain situations may become associated with the onset of an attack. Sometimes the victim does not experience the attack as anxiety, but only as intense physical discomfort.

THE FIRST ATTACK

Ordinarily, patients state that they were caught off guard by their first attack and report that it began suddenly, without warning, from "out of the blue". A panic attack begins with a strange, indescribable, and frightening feeling throughout the body. Immediately thereafter, a rapidly pounding heart draws attention to the chest. As alarm spreads throughout the mind and body, tightness, and sometimes pain in the chest, make breathing difficult. Shortness of breath often leads to gasping or hyperventilation (rapid shallow breathing). If hyperventilation is prominent, it causes dizziness and tingling sensations in the hands or feet (paresthesias). Sweat may break out on the brow and the hands may become moist, cold, and clammy. Sometimes hot flashes or flushing sensations pulsate throughout the entire body, alternating with cold feelings. As fear grips the body, the hands and arms begin to shake and purposeful movements may become difficult. Victims feel that they may faint, go crazy, or lose control. Nausea and abdominal cramping are fairly common, but vomiting is not. If fear and anxiety remain high, the victim may have an "out of the body experience" (depersonalization) or experience feelings of unreality (things look strange or unreal). As these intensely uncomfortable sensations are peaking, thoughts of dying, having a heart attack, or smothering wildly tumble through a victim's mind (see Chart 2). After the attack has passed (usually in a few minutes), the victim is exhausted, confused, scared, and fearful of a recurrence.

AFTER THE ATTACK

A panic attack leaves a fearsome impression on the mind. Questions about the soundness of one's physical or mental health preoccupy the victim long after the panic attack has passed. Concern about the possibility of some underlying physical illness prompts most sufferers to seek an appointment with a physician. In the vast majority of cases, the doctor finds no evidence of physical disease. While this is momentarily reassuring, if another panic attack erupts, doubts reemerge concerning the presence of physical illness or the thoroughness of the doctor's examination. The physician's conclusion that there is nothing seriously wrong collides with the reality of continuing distress. Another visit to the doctor may result in more tests and more reassurance. Doctors who are not familiar with panic disorder may diagnose hypochondriasis (often a code word for crock). And patients may think that the doctor is not too smart (a quack). After all, patients conclude, "If there is nothing seriously wrong with me, why am I continuing to have these awful symptoms?" It seems reasonable for patients to conclude that some undetected disease or malady lurks in their body. The crock/quack impasse connotes a loss of respect between the patient and doctor which must be restored if treatment is to be successful.

CHART 2

THOUGHTS (ENCEPHALIC ACTIVITY) DURING OR AFTER A PANIC ATTACK

1. Thoughts of dying
2. Thoughts of having a heart attack
3. Thoughts of suffocation
4. Thoughts of going out of control
5. Thoughts of going crazy
6. Vague thoughts of impending doom
7. Other thoughts of a cataclysmic nature

Thinking is a mental activity associated with various emotions. Following a panic attack the fearful thoughts listed above often occur and produce additional anxiety. As will be discussed later, the control and eventual elimination of fearful thoughts play an important role during treatment.

FEAR OF PHYSICAL ILLNESS

Very few patients who come into my consulting room report that they are suffering from a panic disorder. Instead, they complain of physical symptoms and suspect an underlying disease. The following clinical vignettes illustrate panic patients who were overly concerned with their physical health.

THE NATIONAL GUARD SOLDIER

A 43-year-old man related that when he was a 22-year-old National Guard soldier protecting state property after a natural disaster, he had a panic attack and collapsed following uninterrupted duty for three days and nights. During the next 20 years, he had numerous panic attacks which resulted in nine hospitalizations and over 20 visits to the emergency room. Although the doctors never found anything wrong with him, he clung tenaciously to the idea that he was physically ill. Past history revealed that at the time of his first attack, he was ambivalently embarking on a marriage and had started a business for which he was ill prepared. During his childhood and adolescence, he suffered from separation anxiety and school phobia and visited many doctors for assorted ailments. Family history revealed that his mother and father had periodic bouts of nervousness. At the time of my examination, the 43-year-old man was experiencing panic attacks two to three times a week, was unhappily married, and was committed to a marginally successful business. It was difficult for him to believe that his panic attacks were not caused by a disease and, after two sessions, he quit treatment to continue his search for a physical cause of his illness.

THE JOGGER

While jogging through the park, a 32-year-old accountant noticed chest pain and believed he was having a heart attack. He stopped, dropped to one knee, and experienced palpitations and panic. Frantically, he flagged down a passing motorist who took him to a hospital. All examinations were normal. When the symptoms continued, the accountant was puzzled. He became more apprehensive and harbored suspicions that he had heart disease. His suspicions grew into an obsession and he stopped jogging because he was convinced that he had something wrong with his heart. A psychiatric evaluation disclosed that the accountant had been under severe stress for the past year due to business and marital problems. He was very concerned about his physical well-being and this was the reason he had begun jogging. Panic disorder was diagnosed and antipanic medication was prescribed for the accountant who also learned techniques of relaxation and thought control (encephalic reconditioning). His panic attacks ceased and anxiety was greatly diminished. He changed his job, improved his marriage, and resumed jogging.

THE WOMAN AND THE SUPERDOME

A 34-year-old woman had her first panic attack in the Superdome, a huge athletic facility in New Orleans. At the time of the panic attack, the woman was having a difficult pregnancy and three weeks later had a miscarriage. Panic attacks persisted as did abdominal complaints. The woman believed that she had cancer or some undiagnosed abdominal ailment. She experienced panic attacks in shopping malls, restaurants and cars, eventually developing agoraphobia. During the psychiatric evaluation, the past history included divorced parents, childhood phobia, and many minor illnesses. Family history disclosed that her mother also suffered from panic attacks. During treatment, an antipanic medication was prescribed and exposure treatment was initiated. The woman's panic attacks stopped, anxiety diminished, and she was desensitized from her phobias. However, deciding she was not a sports enthusiast, she never returned to the Superdome.

Panic patients become obsessed with the erroneous idea that they have physical illness because panic symptoms revolve around various organ systems of the body: heart (cardiovascular), lungs (pulmonary), brain (neurological), and stomach (gastrointestinal). Sometimes symptoms seem so bizarre that patients think they are going crazy (psychiatric disorder). Fear of illness unsubstantiated by objective medical tests often leads to the diagnosis of hypochondriasis (imaginary physical ailment).

FEAR OF HEART ATTACK

When the heart begins to pound rapidly and pain penetrates the chest during a panic attack, it is not unreasonable for victims to conclude that they are having a heart attack. Although physical causes for these symptoms must be considered (Chapter 3), the most common reason for a rapidly beating heart and tightness of the chest (especially in young people) is panic disorder. A recent report by Dr. Frank Kane, Jr. at a meeting of the American Psychiatric Association revealed that thousands of people with perfectly healthy hearts are living the life of "cardiac cripples".

Often, complaints of chest pain are not due to heart disease but reflect untreated panic disorder. Dr. Kane surveyed 371 people who complained of chest pain or other apparent symptoms of heart trouble but showed no sign of heart disease when tested with an angiogram. When questioned, 55 percent were unsure whether they had heart disease, 45 percent figured that exertion would be dangerous, and 32 percent said they were limited in their physical activity. Sixty-nine percent of these patients qualified for the diagnosis of panic or another anxiety disorder. About half of the people in the study were informed that their symptoms were due to stress and anxiety, but only four percent were told to seek mental health treatment and only 17 percent were given antianxiety medication. Of the 540,000 angiograms performed in 1984, up to 45 percent disclosed no sign of heart disease. In 1987, Dr. B. D. Beitman and his colleagues reported that 59 percent of cardiac clinic patients with atypical chest pain had no arteriographic evidence of coronary artery disease but were found to have panic disorder on psychiatric evaluation. These findings clearly indicate that a large number of panic patients believe they have heart disease and do not receive proper treatment for panic disorder.

When the diagnosis of panic disorder is missed, an unhealthy cycle begins. Patients continue to panic and to complain of cardiac symptoms. They consult numerous doctors and receive various diagnoses, but no treatment for panic disorder. And patients keep suffering. After being told that there was nothing wrong with her, one 32-year-old housewife thought to herself, "How can that be true? I am continuing to have these frightening heart palpitations and pain in my chest. There must be something going on with my heart. Why can't the doctors find out what's wrong with me?" Fortunately, most physicians now recognize that cardiac symptoms are part of panic disorder so there need be little confusion about diagnosis.

DIFFICULTIES IN BREATHING

Problems with breathing almost always accompany a panic attack. Tightness of the chest muscles during an attack interferes with easy respiration. Panic patients, however, misinterpret labored breathing as evidence that the lungs will quit working and death will follow. To compensate for the perceived lack of oxygen (there really is none), rapid breathing (hyperventilation) is an almost automatic response. When this happens, the ratio of oxygen and carbon dioxide in the bloodstream changes causing dizziness, feelings of faintness, tingling sensations in the hands, arms, and legs, and occasionally blurred vision. These secondary symptoms which are part of the "hyperventilation syndrome" produce additional alarm. In the patient's mind, difficulties in breathing will lead to asphyxia. I have treated patients who carry valises or large purses containing numerous decongestants, nasal sprays, and a portable bottle of oxygen to combat episodes of shortness of breath. They seldom get used. In panic disorder, smothering sensations indicate anxiety and are not evidence of lung disease. When breathing becomes disordered, however, thoughts about death by suffocation seem as real as a hangman's noose tightening around the neck of a condemned criminal.

STOMACH AND BOWEL COMPLAINTS

During a panic attack, some victims experience abdominal distress. These patients may complain of nausea which is accompanied by a fear of vomiting in public. They avoid eating in restaurants or public places where vomiting may cause embarrassment and humiliation. Other patients who center their attention on their digestive system fear the loss of bowel control and worry about uncontrollable diarrhea. To avoid soiling themselves, they may plan their activities around access to bathrooms. Panic patients who worry about their stomach or bowels rarely vomit or defecate suddenly. Nevertheless, these unfounded fears persist and interfere with attendance at parties, public events, and eating in restaurants. During a panic attack, nausea, extreme abdominal cramping, or feelings of bowel urgency feed the fear of loss of control. Panic disorder patients who fear gastrointestinal symptoms avoid social encounters and professional meetings where food is served. If they attend these functions, they eat little, must have easy access to a bathroom, and do not enjoy themselves.

FEAR OF A BRAIN TUMOR

Some people who suddenly find themselves trembling, shaking, or experiencing dizziness, faintness, blurred vision, unsteadiness, and a fear of losing control think that they have a brain tumor or, at the very least, that something is amiss with their nervous system. A feeling of pressure in the head or severe headaches seemingly confirms the erroneous idea that something must be wrong with the brain. In reality, these cranial symptoms are usually the result of nervous tension due to panic disorder. Other patients with vague symptoms speculate that they may have multiple sclerosis, epilepsy, or some rare neurological disorder. Distressing thoughts about having a brain disease cause additional anxiety which may intensify symptoms. Thinking like a lawyer, some patients conclude that their cranial symptoms are *prima facie* evidence of a brain tumor. The fact that panic and anxiety can simulate some symptoms of a brain disorder is not considered. The onset, type of symptoms, and clinical course of panic disorder clearly distinguish it from an affliction of the nervous system. In the final analysis, panic disorder responds to appropriate treatment, while many maladies of a neurological nature do not.

"Going Crazy"

During a panic attack, a variety of intense, frightening, and fleeting symptoms erupts suddenly, without warning, and for no apparent reason. An "out of body experience" (depersonalization) and a feeling that things look strange or unreal (derealization) stimulate thoughts about losing control, going crazy, and ending up in an insane asylum. A suggestion to consult a psychiatrist may be interpreted by some panic patients that indeed they are losing their mind. Victims may feel that they are going crazy, but they never do. High anxiety, not psychosis, results from a panic attack.

PANIC AND SUICIDE

New data from the "Epidemiological Catchment Area" study, which was published in a 1990 issue of the *New England Journal of Medicine*, has concluded that panic disorder and frequent panic attacks must be added to the list of risk factors for suicide. The study revealed that individuals with panic disorder are at much higher risk for suicidal thoughts and suicidal attempts than those with certain other psychiatric disorders. Among the four groups surveyed, the suicidal attempt rates were: 20 percent - panic disorder; 12 percent - panic attacks; 6 percent - other psychiatric disorders; and, 1 percent - no psychiatric disorder. These findings certainly suggest that both patient and physician should become more aware of suicide as it relates to the diagnosis of panic disorder.

With panic disorder patients, the specific signs and the probability of suicide must be assessed. The development of a suicidal plan and the means to carry out the plan, together with depression and a history of suicidal attempts, are an ominous sign and must be taken very seriously. In panic disorder, thoughts about death do not necessarily represent suicidal ideation. Rather, patients express a concern that some unknown illness will strike them down at any time and at any place. This represents a fear of dying more than a fear of death by one's own hands. When a panic patient attempts suicide, this is a serious act which requires quick intervention by a mental health professional.

Victims of panic disorder sometimes develop what has been called "gun-barrel vision". Seeing no alternatives, the sufferer pessimistically envisions a lifelong series of panic attacks and hopelessly concludes that death is the only solution. When a correct diagnosis of panic disorder has been made and a therapeutic plan formulated, options are widened, allowing the patient hope. As patients improve, suicidal thoughts and attempts should diminish and eventually disappear.

In almost 30 years of clinical practice, I have seen some panic disorder and panic attack patients with suicidal ideation and a few with suicidal gestures, but I have never had a panic disorder patient commit suicide. The "Catchment Area" study focuses attention on the suicidal ideation and suicide attempts of individuals suffering from panic disorder. The authors conclude that although there is no direct evidence to show any treatments (drug and behavioral) will affect suicidal behavior, there is good evidence that they will reduce the frequency of panic attacks and avoidance behavior. It is safe to assume that successfully treated panic patients will be less of a suicidal risk than untreated ones.

PANIC AND THE QUALITY OF LIFE

Panic disorder not only causes individuals to suffer, but it also adversely affects marriage, family, and occupational performance. In panic disorder, pervasive social and health consequences are similar to those found in major depression. In a recent report published in the *Archives of General Psychiatry*, data from the "Epidemiologic Catchment Area" study revealed that both panic disorder and major depression are associated with an increased risk of subjective feelings of poor physical and emotional health. When compared with the general population, panic prone patients are at risk for alcohol and other drug use, suicidal attempts, decreased time on hobbies, poor marital functioning, increased financial dependency, increased use of general medical and/or psychiatric professionals, increased use of tranquilizers, and increased use of hospital emergency departments. Programs of prevention and treatment can do much to enhance the quality of life of panic disorder patients by curtailing personal suffering, improving family and marital relationships, decreasing dependency on alcohol or other drugs, and lowering suicide-related behavior. As patients improve during treatment, their quality of life also begins to improve dramatically.

SUMMARY

Nearly all panic patients have vivid imaginations and dwell on the possible cause of their symptoms. Because panic involves almost every organ system of the body, patients attribute their symptoms to a wide variety of illnesses. As long as panic attacks persist, patients are notoriously resistant to the idea that their symptoms are anxiety-induced and attributable to panic disorder. Panic symptoms are not imaginary, but are the result of anxiety. When panic disorder is properly treated and panic attacks cease, patients will stop blaming their symptoms on physical ailments. Sometimes, panic and anxiety symptoms can be related to medical illness, as will be discussed in the next chapter.

The Old Physician and An Anxious Patient

3

Medical Illness and Panic

While mixing medicine, the old physician notices a look of fear and apprehension on his distraught patient's face. Every doctor, before and since Hippocrates, has known that anxiety accompanies almost all illness. In some medical diseases, anxiety and panic may be the chief symptom. Determining whether anxiety is due to a medical disease or panic disorder requires the skill of a physician. The symptoms and course of each medical disorder usually have distinctive qualities which can be elicited by a careful history. From medical school days, I shall never forget a quote from Sir William Osler, a famous Canadian physician, who said, "Listen to thy patient and he will tell you the diagnosis."

The clinical course of panic disorder is different from most medical illnesses associated with panic and anxiety. In panic disorder, the first attack usually occurs when the patient is in his/her early twenties, but rarely over the age of fifty. The frequency of panic attacks varies from several times a day to twice a month or less. In panic, symptoms are absent or not as intense between attacks and there is usually evidence of a phobia or at least phobic thinking. The medical history, physical examination, and various laboratory tests are ordinarily negative. The Panic Disorder Checklist in the Appendix can also be helpful to sort out panic disorder from medical conditions.

In medical illness, symptoms are usually unrelenting until the disease has run its course. A diagnosis can also be substantiated by the history, physical examination, and various laboratory tests. There is usually no evidence of a phobia or phobic thinking in a medical disorder. This chapter reviews medical disorders which sometimes become confused with panic disorder.

MEDICAL DISORDERS ASSOCIATED WITH PANIC-ANXIETY

When the course of illness suggests a medical disorder, additional examinations are indicated. For example, if a patient complains of panic and nervousness and later has an epileptic seizure, a neurological examination, electroencephalogram (brain wave test), and a special scan of the brain are definitely warranted to rule out a disease of the nervous system. Similarly, disturbances in the cardiovascular (heart), pulmonary (lungs), gastrointestinal (stomach and bowels), and endocrine (hormonal) systems share symptoms with panic disorder (see Chart 3). An electrocardiogram (ECG), chest X-ray, upper and lower GI series, and chemical tests of the blood and urine can help diagnose most existing medical disorders. Panic-like symptoms may also occur during drug and alcohol withdrawal. A careful history, including an interview with a relative or friend, and appropriate laboratory tests can identify substance abusers.

Another issue which separates patients with medical illness from those who have panic disorder is the reaction to their diagnosis. Most patients with a medical problem accept the diagnosis and cooperate with treatment. Panic disorder patients who continue to have panic attacks tend to resist the diagnosis of a mental disorder. It is only when treatment begins to yield results and panic attacks diminish in frequency or stop altogether that patients relinquish the idea of having a physical illness.

CARDIOVASCULAR SYSTEM

About 60 percent of panic patients complain of chest pain. Chest pain should be considered a serious symptom because it may be associated with a heart attack (myocardial infarction) or heart disease (angina pectoris). A careful history can delineate risk factors associated with heart disease such as age, smoking, family history, obesity, etc. An ECG, angiogram, and certain blood tests can detect heart disease.

Pain in the chest may also be due to spasm of the esophagus (the muscular tube leading from the mouth to the stomach), tightness of the chest muscles, or costochondritis (tenderness where the ribs join the breast bone). The latter two conditions may be caused by vigorous exercise or trauma to the chest. Infection involving the lungs can also cause chest pain; however, pneumonia is usually associated with fever and a cough and can be diagnosed by a chest X-ray.

A rapid or irregular heart beat is a common symptom in panic disorder, but occasionally this may indicate a cardiac arrhythmia which can be diagnosed by an ECG. Another cardiac condition, mitral valve prolapse (MVP) is fairly common, occurring in up to 10 percent of the adult population. MVP is ordinarily an innocuous disorder in which the mitral valve pushes into one chamber of the heart (the left atrium) when blood is ejected from the lower chamber (left ventricle). The incidence of MVP in patients with panic disorder ranges from 18 to 27 percent. In identifiable MVP patients, palpitations occur in 50 percent and chest pain in 30 to 50 percent. Although often associated with panic disorder and psychological stress, MVP is considered to be a benign condition which usually does not require treatment. When patients complain of chest pain or rapid irregular heart beat, a thorough history, physical examination, ECG, chest X-ray, and appropriate blood tests must be ordered by a physician. The results of these examinations and tests can differentiate between a cardiovascular condition and panic disorder. Anxious patients with cardiovascular symptoms and a history of fainting or near-fainting episodes should be evaluated by a cardiologist.

THE PULMONARY SYSTEM

Irregularities in breathing may indicate anxiety or lung disease. Respiratory symptoms such as shortness of breath and smothering sensations may be due to asthma, allergic bronchitis, or chronic obstructive pulmonary disease. Pneumonia and pleuritis are usually associated with chest pain and breathing problems; however, fever, a cough, and a pathologic X-ray of the chest usually indicate infection of the lungs. If the history, physical examination, and chest X-ray are inconclusive, additional examinations (a sputum analysis and bronchoscopy) may shed light on the diagnosis. Any tests which show diminishment of vital capacity and pulmonary functioning should make one suspicious of pulmonary pathology. In panic-agoraphobia, disturbance of breathing is anxiety-induced and is not the result of any disease of the lungs.

GASTROINTESTINAL SYSTEM

Gastrointestinal symptoms such as difficulty in swallowing, nausea, vomiting, painful cramps in the abdomen, and diarrhea can be anxiety-related or produced by a myriad of medical conditions. Esophageal spasm and problems in swallowing are most often related to extreme anxiety; sometimes it has a physical cause which can be diagnosed by a visual exam with an appropriate instrument. A gastroscopic examination or upper GI series (swallowing barium and watching its passage through the intestines by X-ray) can detect gastric or duodenal ulcers. A colonoscopic examination can diagnose medical problems in the lower intestinal tract. At times it may be difficult to sort out panic disorder from ordinary gastrointestinal illness. In panic disorder, gastrointestinal symptoms are associated with a panic or limited symptom attack. Few gastrointestinal symptoms are experienced between attacks. In addition, a fear of losing control in social situations (vomiting or defecating unpredictably) is often found in panic disorder. The presence of agoraphobic symptoms also helps distinguish panic disorder from medical causes of gastrointestinal problems.

NEUROLOGICAL SYSTEM

Recurrent panic attacks and anxiety are prominent in organic anxiety syndrome. This condition can be caused by intoxication with certain drugs (caffeine, cocaine, and amphetamines) or withdrawal from alcohol or other sedative type drugs. Tumors in certain parts of the brain and epilepsy are not common but can cause organic anxiety syndrome. An organic mental disorder with anxiety may also be caused by head trauma, especially if it was followed by a long period of unconsciousness. Symptoms of light-headedness, a fear of loosing control, fainting and dizziness should always be explored to rule out any abnormality of the central nervous system.

Temporal lobe epilepsy and partial seizures have been associated with panic attacks. Patients with epilepsy also complain of depersonalization, derealization, and display extreme irritability, aggressiveness, and a personality change. A person suffering from partial or focal seizures exhibits motor, sensory, or psychomotor phenomena which are not present during a typical panic attack.

A tumor, epilepsy, and other organic mental disorders can be ruled out by an X-ray, CT scan, magnetic resonance imaging (MRI), or an electroencephalogram. If toxic substances, drugs, or hormonal abnormalities cause an organic anxiety syndrome, these substances can easily be detected by blood and urine tests. Panic attacks and anxiety, occurring in conjunction with a neurological disease or organic mental disorder, are not accompanied by phobic thinking or a phobia. In the final analysis, objective tests of brain functioning differentiates the panic attack associated with panic disorder from the one produced by a neurological disease.

Vertigo may be associated with brain disease. However, if the neurological examination is negative, vertigo raises a suspicion of a vestibular abnormality, possibly labyrinthitis or some other inner ear problem. An otologic examination by a specialist is simple and can rule out any inner ear disorder. Dizziness is a common symptom in panic disorder and also a side effect of certain types of medication. Light-headedness can also be caused by low blood pressure, especially when hypotensive people stand up suddenly. If physical examination and other tests are negative, the most common reason for dizziness is anxiety.

ENDOCRINE DISORDERS

Disturbance in levels of hormones can produce symptoms similar to anxiety and panic. Hyperthyroidism, for example, may be associated with nervousness, tremor of the hands, sweating, sensitivity to heat, rapid heart beat, fatigue, and diarrhea. The presence of a goiter and certain eye characteristics including stare, lid retraction, and protrusion of the eyes suggest thyroid disease. A blood serum analysis measuring thyroid hormones can clearly establish or reject the diagnosis of hyperthyroidism.

A tumor of the adrenal gland is relatively rare, but it can be associated with rapid heart beat, difficulties in breathing, hot and cold feelings, headaches, chest pain, nausea, vomiting, abdominal pain, and a sense of impending doom. The tumor excretes excessive amounts of epinephrine and norepinephrine (anxiety producing hormones) which can easily be detected by testing the urine. In addition, alterations in blood pressure are common, and about half of the patients have high blood pressure.

Variations in blood sugar level have been associated with anxiety. Nervousness, palpitations, sweating, tremors, faintness, headaches, and visual disturbance are often found in patients with low blood sugar. Hypoglycemia is also associated with symptoms of hunger, muscle weakness, staggering gait, and in severe cases, loss of consciousness and convulsions. These same symptoms can be found in diabetics who take too much insulin (hyperinsulinism). Any alterations in blood sugar level can be detected by means of a simple blood sugar test or glucose tolerance test. Hypoglycemia was a popular diagnosis a few decades ago, but is now considered to be a relatively uncommon cause for panic and anxiety symptoms.

Another rare condition which can simulate some symptoms of panic disorder is hypoparathyroidism. The parathyroid hormone controls calcium metabolism, and low levels of this hormone cause a low calcium level in the bloodstream. Symptoms of hypoparathyroidism include: tingling sensations, muscular cramps, and spasm in the hands or feet. The presence of the foregoing symptoms and a low level of calcium in the bloodstream confirm the diagnosis.

Sometimes alteration of female hormones during menopause produces sweating, flushes, chills, and anxiety. Menopause, of course, occurs mainly in older females, and the age at onset of symptoms helps make the diagnosis. Luteal phase disorder (LPD), formerly called premenstrual syndrome, is also hormonal-related. Symptoms occur a week before and a few days after the onset of menses. Symptoms of LPD include: marked anxiety, tension, irritability, anger, headaches, fatigue, joint or muscle pain, difficulties in concentration, and insomnia. LPD may also be associated with depression and interfere with work, social, and recreational activities. Ordinarily, the symptoms of LPD remit with the onset of menses, while those of panic disorder do not. The absence of phobic avoidance and phobic thinking also differentiates LPD from panic disorder.

CHART 3

MEDICAL DISORDERS ASSOCIATED WITH ANXIETY

Cardiovascular System
    Myocardial Infarct
    Angina Pectoris
    Cardiac Arrhythmia
    Mitral Valve Prolapse

Pulmonary System
    Asthma
    Allergic Bronchitis
    Chronic Obstructive Pulmonary Disease
    Pneumonia

Gastrointestinal System
    Esophageal Spasm
    Hiatal Hernia
    Gastric or Peptic Ulcer
    Colitis
    Other Gastrointestinal Abnormalities

Neurological System
    Temporal Lobe Epilepsy
    Partial Seizures
    Brain Tumor
    Organic Anxiety Syndrome

Endocrine Disorders
    Hyperthyroidism
    Pheochromocytoma (Tumor of Adrenal Gland)
    Hypoglycemia
    Hypoparathyroidism
    Hyperinsulinism
    Menopause
    Luteal Phase Disorder

SUMMARY

Some symptoms of panic disorder suggest a physical disease. For this reason, it is important to uncover any underlying disease by a thorough physical examination and appropriate laboratory tests. Because anxiety-related symptoms are often misinterpreted as evidence of physical illness, sufferers should request a careful explanation of significant symptoms and their relationship to panic disorder from their doctor. After a normal physical examination, some physicians tell panic patients that nothing is wrong with them. The correct conclusion is, "There is something wrong with you — panic disorder; however, you do not have any serious or underlying physical disease." In this way, patients will not be surprised when symptoms of panic-anxiety continue for awhile during the initial stages of treatment. The suspicion of physical illness disappears only when the patient begins to improve and anxiety-related symptoms diminish or disappear.

Part II

Agoraphobia — Avoiding Panic

The Phobic Greek

4

The Phobic Greek

Agora is the Greek word for market place. If you visit an ancient Greek ruin, your tour guide may point out a large, open space and tell you that this was the agora. With some imagination, you can see the tents and stalls where the merchants are selling their wares. Amphoras filled with wine or olive oil, racks of lamb, various fruits, clothing, and jewelry are to be seen everywhere. The agora is probably crowded with people looking at these goods, bargaining with the merchants, and discussing politics, while different animals mill about. There is excitement and controlled chaos within the agora. Now, imagine an ancient Greek having a panic attack amidst the crowded and confused confines of the agora. Exit is difficult because of the mass of people, the number of stalls, and the wandering animals. The Greek becomes more anxious and panic-stricken as he attempts to leave the busy agora to seek help or to go home. A close friend may notice the look of fear on the Greek's face and ask, "What is wrong?" "I feel sick," is the likely reply and the friend assists the stricken Greek home where the anxiety symptoms subside. On the next visit to the agora, the Greek begins to feel anxious and panicky and quickly returns home. Eventually, he refuses to go to the agora and may even balk at visits to other people's homes, preferring the sanctuary of his own house. The Greek has panic disorder and is phobic of the agora.

HISTORY OF AGORAPHOBIA

The syndrome of agoraphobia was studied long before panic disorder was described. In 1871 the German physician, Westphal, suggested the name "agoraphobia" for a disorder in which the patient experienced anxiety while walking alone across open spaces or through empty streets. With a keen eye, characteristic of nineteenth century physicians, Westphal also noted that in agoraphobia, anxiety symptoms were more prominent when patients were sitting in a church, the theater, or standing in large rooms where many people were gathered. He also observed that anxiety was alleviated by the presence of a companion, when the patient was distracted, carried an umbrella, or drank alcohol.

In 1870, Dr. V. Benedikt, described a similar malady, but he believed that the key symptom was dizziness rather than anxiety. Benedikt labeled the condition "platzschwindel" (dizziness in public places). Another physician, Dr. E. Cordes, in 1871 described cases similar to those reported by Westphal and Benedikt. Cordes' careful clinical observations led him to conclude that anxiety was based as much on ideas of the mind as it was on the environment. The notion that thinking could generate anxiety was new and would not emerge in psychiatry until much later with the development of cognitive therapy (changing the videotapes of the mind), as will be discussed in a later chapter. Cordes also described his patients' physical symptoms of palpitations, nausea, headache, pressure in the chest, breathlessness, and a fear when in crowds.

In 1890, Dr. S. W. Clevenger wrote about a case of panphobia in the journal *The Alienist and Neurologist*. Written in the first person, this wonderfully detailed account of a patient suffering from what we now would call agoraphobia follows:

A sense of impending danger seemed to descend, spoiling every pleasure, thwarting every ambition. The dread of sudden death, which was at first marked, gradually subsided, giving way more to a feeling of dread — not of dying suddenly — but of doing so under peculiar circumstances or away from home. I became morbidly sensitive about being brought into close contact with any large number of people. Finding myself in the midst of a large gathering would inspire a feeling of terror (which)...could be relieved in but one way — by getting away from the spot as soon as possible. Acting on this impulse I have left churches, theatres, even funerals, simply because of an utter inability to control myself to stay. For 10 years I have not been to church, to the theatre, to political gatherings or any form of popular meeting, except where I could remain in the background, with means of egress convenient. Even at my mother's funeral . . . I was utterly unable to bring myself to sit with the other members of the family in the front of the church. Not only has this unfortunate trait deprived me of an immense amount of pleasure and benefit, but it has also been a matter of considerable expense . . . . Time more than I can recall I have gone into restaurants or dining rooms, ordered a meal and left it untouched, impelled by my desire to escape the crowd . . . . I have . . . often . . . walked long distances — perhaps a mile — to avoid crossing some pasture or open square, even when it was a matter of moment to me to save all the time possible . . . . This malady . . . has throttled all ambition, and killed all personal pride, spoiled every pleasure . . . over this the will seems to have no control.

For many years, agoraphobia was not well understood. It was a condition that defied treatment and was easy to misdiagnose. Physical symptoms suggested a medical illness and usually directed the patient to their general practitioner. Failure to find a physical cause for fears and anxiety often led to protracted suffering or to a psychiatrist's couch for many years of fruitless treatment for a "neurosis". It was only when agoraphobia was conceived as a phobic reaction to periodic panic attacks that effective biological and psychological treatment developed.

DEFINITION OF AGORAPHOBIA

Fear of the agora or market place is a common definition of agoraphobia. It is true that contemporary patients develop a phobia of the modern equivalent of the agora, the suburban shopping center, but this is an incomplete definition. A more comprehensive definition of agoraphobia includes three important parts: (1) the fear of having a panic attack, (2) a phobia secondary to panic attacks, and (3) the evolution of phobic thinking (see Chart 4).

Fear of a panic attack, or what has been described as a "fear of fear", is primary. In most cases, panic attacks do not occur on a daily basis, but high anxiety does. The presence of above normal levels of anxiety keeps alive the thought that a panic attack might strike at any time.

The second part of agoraphobia can be observed by most anyone - the phobic reaction of avoidance. Because of the fear of having a panic attack, victims withdraw to a safe place where help might be available. Places where they feel "trapped" are avoided, and activities associated with a panic attack are evaded.

A third characteristic of agoraphobia involves an unhealthy mental habit called phobic or catastrophic thinking. In part, phobic thinking is an anxiety-evoking self-statement, usually beginning with the phrase, "What will happen if . . . ?" and ending with a possible, but highly improbable dangerous consequence. Phobic thinking also involves the prediction of a bad outcome to ordinary life events. When considering any activity, anxiety-evoking thoughts pop up in the mind and contribute to the phobic reaction of avoidance. These dire thoughts raise anxiety but rarely come true. Phobic thinking is self-defeating and makes cowards out of courageous people.

CHART 4

COMPONENTS OF AGORAPHOBIA

1. Fear of having a panic attack
2. Phobic reaction of avoidance
3. Phobic thinking

AGORAPHOBIA AND PANIC

Without panic, agoraphobia probably would not develop. The sudden onset of an emotionally painful attack, followed in a few seconds by a strong discharge from the nervous system and intense symptoms of anxiety, makes most people "scared to death". After an attack, victims ask themselves, "What has happened to me? What is wrong with me? What caused this? Will it happen again? Will I die, go crazy, or lose control?" The frightening symptoms and sensations in the body are not imaginary and not easy to forget. The possibility of having another panic attack begins to dominate the mind and governs future behavior.

Even when panic attacks do not erupt frequently, victims become over-alerted to danger and notice with alarm any change in bodily sensations suggestive of another attack. Dizziness, irregularities in breathing or heart beat, and other symptoms associated with the first attack cause an escalation of anxiety and a fear of having another panic attack. This "limited symptom attack" has the same effect as a full-blown panic attack. Victims feel that there is something terribly wrong with them and fear for their lives and sanity. In the final analysis, it matters little whether the victim fears a full-blown panic attack or a "small panic attack" (limited symptom attack). The result is the same — abnormally high levels of anxiety during most of the day. Any additional anxiety caused by problems of everyday living elevates apprehension and increases the fear of having an attack. For example, anxiety due to difficulties at work, marital conflicts, or financial problems is added to existing anxiety increasing the probability of having a panic attack. After a while, the possibility of having a panic attack dominates thinking and interferes with the resolution of problems not related to panic. In a highly anxious state, the victim's main priority becomes the lowering of anxiety. To achieve this end, the sufferer discovers by trial and error or happenstance that refuge in a "safe haven" lowers anxiety, thus setting up the phobic reaction of avoidance.

THE PHOBIC REACTION — AVOIDANCE

Most people have a phobia of some sort. Johnny Carson of *The Tonight Show* delights in telling audiences about his phobia of backing into a doorknob. Some of us are superstitious and avoid walking under ladders, crossing the path of a black cat, or using the number 13. A phobia must be distinguished from superstition or aversion resulting from distaste or dislike. The phobic reaction of avoidance is always associated with a reduction in anxiety, while avoidance because of superstition, dislike, or distaste involves only movement away from an unpleasant situation.

Phobic persons have two options in regard to their problem. They may stay in the phobic place and suffer or escape the anxiety-evoking situation. Avoidance appears to be a natural reaction to fear and anxiety; however, the phobic reaction of avoidance always restricts freedom of movement and causes additional problems. By definition, a phobic reaction is an irrational choice. Worse yet, the lowering of anxiety associated with avoidance tends to perpetuate maladaptive phobic behavior. In a sense, a phobic person is rewarded for escaping from the phobic situation.

AGORAPHOBIA AND AVOIDANCE

In agoraphobia, the phobic reaction of avoidance assumes major proportions and interferes with almost every aspect of daily living. When agoraphobics attempt to cope with panic and anxiety, they discover that the quickest and easiest way to reduce these uncomfortable feelings is to return home or to seek the company of a trusted person. Anxiety is the misguided navigator, directing the agoraphobic towards places and situations where immediate comfort is achieved. This maneuver represents an almost reflexive action and is not a reasoned analysis of the best thing to do. Unfortunately, the decrease of anxiety reinforces phobic behavior, resulting in more and more avoidance with a loss of personal freedom.

Most agoraphobic patients are not aware that leaving a phobic situation rewards or reinforces that behavior. After all, the agoraphobic may rationalize, "Don't most people avoid potentially dangerous situations?" Omitted from this rhetorical question is the fact that in agoraphobia there *is* no realistic danger. Agoraphobics do experience episodes of panic-anxiety which admittedly are uncomfortable but not life-threatening. The phobic reaction of avoidance restricts choices and is not adaptive. For example, if an agoraphobic goes to a shopping mall and begins to experience panic-anxiety, avoidance does decrease symptoms. It also interferes with the purchase of needed items and deprives one of a potentially pleasurable outing. The shopping mall offers no realistic danger and leaving it reinforces the tendency to flee, making it more difficult to return the next time. Eventually, just thinking about going to a shopping mall (phobic thinking) raises anxiety sufficient to inhibit shopping.

PHOBIC THINKING

One's style of thinking is like any other activity or habit, only it is not visible. Some people have the habit of thinking optimistically and positively and seem always to have a cheery outlook. Still others, who appear morose and depressed, often think about gloomy and pessimistic things. In agoraphobia, almost all sufferers have developed the anxiety-evoking habit of phobic or catastrophic thinking. In part, phobic thinking consists of irrational ideas and fearful thoughts about danger to self. Thinking about having a panic attack and speculating about a bad outcome to an ordinary life event increases anxiety. Sometimes phobic thinking generates so much anxiety that it inhibits any action. For example, before going on a vacation, to a party, or to other social or recreational events, phobic thinking may increase anxiety to the point that these activities are avoided.

The "what if . . ." or "what will happen if . . ." self-statements, followed by some frightening but highly unlikely possibilities, typify phobic thinking in agoraphobia. Examples include: "What will happen if I . . . go on an airplane and it crashes? . . . drive my car and have an accident? . . . get into an elevator and it stalls between floors? . . . go shopping and have a heart attack?"

The important concept to remember is that thinking is an active physiologic process which produces feelings and emotions related to behavior. Thus, what we think determines how we feel. How we feel determines, to a large extent, what we do, that is, how we behave.

Because of the tendency to presage panic (an example of phobic thinking), anxiety peaks at relatively high levels throughout the day. This apprehensive expectation is associated with the following symptoms of generalized anxiety: motor tension (trembling, shaky feelings, muscle tension, head-

aches, fatigue), autonomic hyperactivity (shortness
of breath, palpitations or increased heart rate, sweating, dizziness, gastrointestinal symptoms, frequent
urination, lump in the throat, trouble swallowing),
and increased vigilance and scanning (feeling on
edge, nervousness, difficulties concentrating, insomnia, and irritability). Symptoms of generalized
anxiety feed the habit of phobic thinking, which in
turn heightens the fear of having a panic attack. Most
of the time phobics are unaware of the pernicious
habit of phobic thinking because it seems normal.
After panic attacks have occurred, increased vigilance
seems appropriate. Phobic thinking is a bad habit
which must be dealt with directly during treatment.

BACKGROUND OF AGORAPHOBICS

Various studies have implicated family instability
and maternal over-protectiveness as causative factors
in the development of agoraphobia. Insecurity during the early years is certainly a common occurrence.
Overly-protected children, tied to the apron strings,
are shy, fearful, and inhibited; the condition has been
described as "separation anxiety". Children with
separation anxiety, according to the *Diagnostic and
Statistical Manual of Mental Disorders* of the
American Psychiatric Association, usually exhibit some
of the following symptoms and behaviors: (1) excessive worry about possible harm befalling one's mother
or other significant figure, (2) unrealistic and excessive worry about untoward calamitous events, (3)
school phobia, (4) reluctance or refusal to sleep

alone, (5) fearfulness when alone, (6) nightmares involving separation from mother or other significant figure, (7) physical complaints, (8) fear and anxiety when anticipating separation from mother or home, and (9) complaints of excessive distress when separated from mother or home.

Dr. Jerome Kagan of Harvard University has observed a behavioral pattern in infants and young children which he termed "behavioral inhibition to the unfamiliar". Infants in this group displayed sleeplessness, irritability, a tendency to colic, marked behavioral restraint, and anxiety in novel situations. These characteristics in infants and young children may lead to the development of anxiety disorders later in life, Dr. Kagan suggests. It may be possible to identify those children with behavioral inhibition to the unfamiliar and plan programs of prevention to diminish the risk for the development of an anxiety disorder.

As early as kindergarten or even before, a child may display an excessive fear reaction or panic when left at school or at a neighbor's house. Difficulties in concentration often result in poor school performance. The teacher may report to the parents that their child is high-strung or nervous and may recommend counseling. Complaints of physical illness are common, resulting in visits to a doctor with increased attention from the mother. Sometimes a child may feign physical illness to avoid going to school. A fear of abandonment characterizes "separation anxiety" and may predispose the child to agoraphobia.

The susceptible adolescent is anxious, complains of physical symptoms, and may experience a panic attack. Visits to doctors disclose no evidence of physical illness. A perceptive physician, noting emotional instability, may refer the adolescent to a social worker or psychiatrist. Sometimes the symptoms of agoraphobia crystallize and progress during adolescence, and the youngster becomes housebound. More often, however, fears smolder and the phobic reaction of avoidance is sporadic. Many adult agoraphobic patients state that during adolescence they were nervous, unsure of themselves, concerned with their physical health, socially awkward, and not happy.

Many of the patients that I have treated for agoraphobia share a common history in which experiences during early developmental years have over-alerted them to danger. Comparative studies have demonstrated that agoraphobic patients were more anxious, had more physical symptoms related to anxiety, more depression, were less assertive, and felt more powerless and helpless than non-agoraphobics. Agoraphobics also have a tendency to mislabel internal (endogenous) cues and to respond with fear more to internal than to external (environmental) stimuli.

Obviously, most people with insecure backgrounds do not develop agoraphobia; hence, we must search for additional factors. There is a definite link between panic and agoraphobia. In panic there is a strong hereditary component which is related to brain functioning. Since the onset of panic disorder occurs most frequently between the ages of 18 and 35, one can assume that the brain is peculiarly sensitive at this time, possibly because of a developmental lag. When a panic attack strikes, victims do their best to cope with the severe symptoms. Based on previous experience with fear and anxiety, coping consists of withdrawal to a safe and secure place (phobic avoidance). Most likely, this avoidance behavior was learned during early developmental years by children who were over-alerted to danger and sought safety at home near mother. Agoraphobia can then be seen as a defense mechanism to shield victims from the uncomfortable effects of panic and high anxiety. The phobic reaction of avoidance does work effectively to lower anxiety; however, it is unsatisfactory. Because no actual danger or threat to survival exists, avoidance wastes time and limits activities. Nevertheless, people who have panic attacks and develop agoraphobia use this maneuver of avoidance to lower anxiety without considering the consequences.

TRAPPED BY PANIC

Agoraphobics shun those places where they feel "trapped" and where escape is not easy. Uncertainty about panic attacks results in an avoidance or reluctance to go places which require attendance for a specific period of time. For example, after placing an order with a waiter in a restaurant, agoraphobics feel "trapped" because they must wait for the food to be prepared and served. It is inappropriate to leave the restaurant before that time, and it is especially difficult if other people are seated at the table. Under these conditions, agoraphobics feel very nervous, have a poor appetite, and in general feel miserable. Occasionally, if anxiety begins to build to a high level, an excuse is made and the agoraphobic leaves the restaurant before the meal is served. Needless to say, the premature ending of dinner can create conflicts with the non-agoraphobic spouse and puzzle dining companions. Other "trapped" situations include concerts, church services, or public meetings. These activities are usually avoided unless the agoraphobic can sit at the rear, near the aisle and exit, so quick escape is possible if feelings of high anxiety and impending panic occur. The more unpredictable the situation, the higher the anxiety, and the greater the reluctance to attend. Waiting in the checkout lane at a supermarket represents another "trapped" situation, and shopping carts filled with groceries may be abandoned as anxiety climbs prior to payment. Driving in heavy traffic or on expressways may also be avoided as agoraphobics fear being stalled in a traffic jam. Trapped by panic is no euphemism, but is a reality encountered daily by most agoraphobic patients.

Severe Agoraphobia

5

Fearful and Housebound

Fearful and housebound, agoraphobics may as well be peering from behind the bars of a jail. Worse than serving time in a penitentiary, agoraphobia imprisons not only the body, but also the mind. Like a computer which has been misprogrammed, the mind plays dirty tricks on the body, signaling danger when no real danger exists. Although agoraphobics experience occasional panic attacks, they are self-limited, pass quickly, and pose no threat to life or limb. Nevertheless, the misinformed mind orders the body to seek refuge from panic symptoms. This affords immediate easement from anxiety, but a price is paid. Similar to a Faustian pact, panic-prone patients promise that they will not venture forth unaccompanied if the devil (panic) abates. This satanic contract sacrifices personal autonomy for immediate anxiety relief. Like any bad bargain, the compact always works to an agoraphobic's disadvantage. Anxiety persists, sufferers remain fearful, and may even become housebound. The real culprit, Pan, the god of panic, must be confronted directly. Anxiety, the co-conspirator, must also be dealt with in order to break the self-imprisoning covenant.

Being housebound is the stereotype of agoraphobia and implies severe mental incapacity bordering on craziness. Books, newspaper articles, and programs on television have characterized agoraphobia as a bizarre disorder. An inability to leave home unaccompanied conjures visions of a hermit or a helpless, dependent recluse. The sudden, sporadic eruption of panic symptoms, suggesting physical illness in one who looks to be the picture of health, is puzzling. Fearful and housebound, the agoraphobic presents a weird spectacle to the casual observer.

Actually, the popular picture of agoraphobia represents the severe form of the disorder which occurs only in a minority of cases. Most patients are not housebound and manage to cope in varying degrees with periodic panic attacks and high anxiety. In mild and moderate cases of agoraphobia, the symptoms are not obvious; however, lifestyle is restricted. Careful inquiry reveals anxiety, physical complaints, and some impairment in work, marriage, interpersonal relationships, and pleasure. If mental health professionals do not obtain a detailed history, the mild and moderate cases of agoraphobia may be overlooked.

MILD AGORAPHOBIA

In the mildest form of agoraphobia, only the spouse or a very close relative or friend may be aware of any incapacity (see Chart 5). There is a history of panic attacks, but they do not occur frequently. The phobic reaction of avoidance is minimal. Phobic thinking, however, develops after the first few panic attacks and begins to dominate the mind. In mild cases, anxiety or fear is always present, but this emotional discomfort is tolerated. Physical symptoms due to anxiety cause a preoccupation with health, though not an obsessive one. Victims may leave home unaccompanied; however, travel is viewed with caution and apprehension.

Mild agoraphobics carefully structure their lives to minimize anxiety. To avoid becoming "trapped" between exits, they might drive to work using a route that excludes expressways. If possible, mild agoraphobics detour around bridges and streets with heavy traffic, preferring service roads or areas of the city where traffic is minimal. They suffer mild anxiety when working, shopping, visiting friends, entering into social situations, or going to new places. Agoraphobics with the mild form of the disorder have a tendency to avoid nonessential activities and certain places previously associated with a panic attack.

Because panic attacks are infrequent, mild agoraphobics may never seek treatment. Adjustments are made in lifestyle, and friends are persuaded to accommodate to any restrictions imposed by anxiety.

CHART 5

MILD AGORAPHOBIA

	1. Not Present	2. Sometimes	3. Often	4. Very Often	5. Almost Always
1. Panic Attacks or Fear of Having One		X			
2. Phobic Reaction (Avoidance)		X			
3. Phobic Thinking			X		
4. Complaints of Physical Symptoms			X		
5. Conflicts with Family Members or Marriage Problems	X				
6. Work Impairment	X				
7. Lack of Participation in Social/Recreational Activities		X			
8. Impaired Interpersonal Relationships		X			
9. Depression	X				
10. Being Housebound	X				

Sometimes, the phobic reaction of avoidance may be disguised. A refusal to participate in social activities or to travel to certain places is explained as a dislike. For example, those with mild agoraphobia may reject an invitation to attend athletic events, professing that they do not like sports. In reality, they want to avoid the anxious "trapped feeling" many agoraphobics have while sitting in the enclosure of a stadium.

Even when they appear in a doctor's office, mild agoraphobics show symptoms which can often be mistaken for a number of medical conditions, including psychosomatic illness or free floating anxiety. It is difficult to estimate how many are suffering from this anxiety disorder in the United States. One can only guess that of the 13.1 million Americans suffering from anxiety disorders, a sizeable percentage must suffer from mild agoraphobia.

MODERATE AGORAPHOBIA

Increased frequency of panic attacks worsens agoraphobia. Panic attacks, in a sense, are the driving force which intensifies symptoms and pushes the patient into a more severe and incapacitating form of this disorder. To escape from the perceived consequence of panic, the phobic reaction of avoidance becomes more pervasive.

Although not housebound, moderate agoraphobics experience more intense anxiety, avoid more situations and places, and progressively have a more restricted lifestyle. Phobic thinking in the form of presaging panic and anticipating anxiety, intensifies symptoms and consumes more time. Physical complaints which are anxiety based also increase and heighten concern for well-being. Family relationships, especially in marriage, begin to deteriorate as irrational requests promote more dependency. Spouses and families are forced to reject or comply with the agoraphobic's unreasonable demands. For instance, the moderate agoraphobic may refuse to attend church, the movies, or any event where they may feel "trapped". To go out or not to go out is a dilemma which places a strain on marital and family relationships. Disagreements between the spouse and the agoraphobic victim cause additional anxiety, which in turn increases the phobic reaction of avoidance and fosters more opportunities for conflict. This vicious cycle complicates the treatment of agoraphobia.

In moderate agoraphobia, a breakdown in interpersonal relationships is more noticeable. Diminished involvement in social and recreational activities isolates agoraphobics from friends and leisure. Embarrassment about symptoms and irrational behavior causes most agoraphobics to maintain the secrecy of their disorder, further increasing isolation. If friends are let in on the secret, they are usually enlisted to provide unhealthy emotional support, thus reinforcing symptoms and dependency. For example, while driving to a social event, a friend may be told of an impending panic attack followed by a request to drive back home. The friend, unaware of the nature of agoraphobia, complies and this act of kindness serves only to perpetuate the phobia and increase disability. As life becomes more constricted, the agoraphobic sinks into despondency and, in many cases, clinical depression.

More frequent panic attacks, or the fear of them, draw a victim's attention towards bodily sensations. Those with moderate agoraphobia develop anxiety-produced physical symptoms which suggest disease. As a consequence, medical consultation is frequently sought. Failure to connect the onset of symptoms to a panic attack and overlooking the phobic reaction of avoidance are common reasons for a misdiagnosis. Depending on the chief complaint, the patient suffering from moderate agoraphobia may be inappropriately diagnosed and treated for a number of medical conditions.

If the doctor notes anxiety as the chief symptom, a referral to a psychiatrist may be recommended. Psychiatrists usually make the correct diagnosis of panic disorder, but sometimes do not recognize agoraphobia. In over 25 years of psychiatric practice, I have seen agoraphobia misdiagnosed all too often. Occasionally, the meaningless diagnosis of "diffuse or free-floating anxiety" is made instead of panic disorder with agoraphobia. Since many agoraphobics are females (three to one over males), and some women are excitable and dramatically present their symptoms, an incorrect diagnosis of hysterical or histrionic personality is not uncommon. When a history of school phobia or separation anxiety is connected to increased dependency upon others, dependent personality disorder may be proffered to explain agoraphobic symptoms. Borderline personality disorder, manic-depressive disorder, and even schizophrenia have been incorrectly applied to patients that I have seen in consultation. Whereas symptoms of mild agoraphobia can be ignored or judged to be inconsequential, the symptomatology in moderate agoraphobia cannot easily be pushed aside (see Chart 6).

Although persons with moderate agoraphobia can leave home unescorted, restrictions in travel are almost always present. A refusal to drive at night or

---

CHART 6

MODERATE AGORAPHOBIA

	1. Not Present	2. Sometimes	3. Often	4. Very Often	5. Almost Always
1. Panic Attack or Fear of Having One			X	to	X
2. Phobic Reaction (Avoidance)			X		
3. Phobic Thinking				X	
4. Complaints of Physical Symptoms				X	
5. Conflicts with Family Members or Marriage Problems			X	to X	
6. Work Impairment			X		
7. Lack of Participation in Social/Recreational Activities			X	to X	
8. Impaired Interpersonal Relationships			X		
9. Depression			X		
10. Being Housebound			X	to X	

in unfamiliar areas of the city is common. Riding in vehicles (buses, trains, airplanes) which are under the control of a stranger is avoided if possible. The moderate agoraphobic tends to avoid public events including church functions, the theater, athletic contests, or other gatherings. Moderate agoraphobia greatly affects one's lifestyle and places much stress upon sufferers and their families. Although they do not usually quit work, job performance can be impaired.

The moderate agoraphobic may not be completely candid about the reasons for limitations in lifestyle. Instead, rationalization may become an inadequate way of coping. Sufferers may deny any incapacity and, if confronted, may insist that they are not victims of agoraphobia because they can still leave home unaccompanied. Down deep, however, they do realize that something is really wrong.

SEVERE AGORAPHOBIA

The classic agoraphobic syndrome is the severe type which is characterized by being housebound. It takes no expert to make the correct diagnosis. Victims are extremely fearful and refuse to leave home unless accompanied by someone that they trust. When home alone, the severe agoraphobic feels queazy and quite nervous. In some cases they require a sitter in attendance at all times. In severe agoraphobia, disability is great, affecting almost all areas of life (see Chart 7).

Panic attacks occur more frequently in severe agoraphobia and the fear of having one is correspondingly high. The phobic reaction of avoidance restricts autonomous living and results in increased dependency and houseboundedness. Phobic thinking dominates the mind and generates extremely high levels of anxiety. Whenever severe agoraphobics think about leaving home, even with a trusted friend, the presaging of panic and the anticipation of anxiety ensures an uncomfortable outing. Phobic thinking supplants most other thoughts, leaving victims little time to contemplate pleasurable things.

Frequent monitoring of bodily sensations heightens fear, and victims become self-absorbed with the idea of physical illness. This does not necessarily lead to a doctor's office. In some cases, the doctor may be ensnared in the phobic reaction and avoided. Unlike physically ill people who eagerly seek a physician's care and cooperate with treatment, severe agoraphobics may resist therapy. Sensitivity to bodily sensations is so great that they may refuse to take prescription drugs which have side effects because of the fear that medication will precipitate a panic attack. Doctors become perplexed when patients refuse to take medication, precipitously cancel appointments, or fail to comply with treatment recommendations. They misinterpret this behavior as recalcitrance rather than the real cause — fear.

Not only is the severe agoraphobic imprisoned by symptoms, but their marriage also becomes enmeshed in the disorder. When one spouse becomes dysfunctional, the balance of the marital relationship shifts.

The agoraphobic assumes an overly dependent role and conflicts always arise. What does a spouse do when a loved one is suffering and appears helpless? It would seem that the correct answer is straightforward — consult a therapist or doctor. However, this obvious solution is not always implemented. To alleviate suffering, the healthy spouse complies with requests which on the surface make no sense. Invariably, the well spouse falls into the "agoraphobic trap" and goes along with irrational requests, thereby increasing dependency. As the marital relationship becomes more and more one-sided, love, friendship, and mutual pleasure diminish. Divorce may result unless appropriate therapy is instituted.

In severe agoraphobia, being housebound interferes markedly with ordinary life events. Leaving home each morning to go to work becomes almost impossible. Unemployment can be a consequence of severe agoraphobia. Prior to treatment, some of my patients have found work which can be done at home, including: telephone sales, typing, computer programming, or architectural drafting. Other agoraphobics, who own their own businesses, can structure their time and hire people to do leg-work outside the home. I am always amazed by the ingenuity of some severe agoraphobic patients to conduct work within the constraints imposed by houseboundedness. Housewives who cannot shop, pick up children from school, or conduct business outside of the home must make alternative arrangements. Simple tasks become difficult, and it is no wonder that many severe agoraphobics become depressed.

CHART 7

SEVERE AGORAPHOBIA

	1. Not Present	2. Sometimes	3. Often	4. Very Often	5. Almost Always
1. Panic Attack or Fear of Having One				X to	X
2. Phobic Reaction (Avoidance)				X to	X
3. Phobic Thinking					X
4. Complaints of Physical Symptoms				X to	X
5. Conflicts with Family Members or Marriage Problems					X
6. Work Impairment				X to	X
7. Lack of Participation in Social/Recreational Activities				X to	X
8. Impaired Interpersonal Relationships				X to	X
9. Depression				X	
10. Being Housebound					X

AGORAPHOBIA AND DEPRESSION

Depression is frequently a secondary manifestation of agoraphobia. The agoraphobic syndrome greatly restricts one's freedom and forces change in lifestyle. Ordinary tasks like leaving home or performing daily duties require more time and energy. The threat of a panic attack looms large and interferes with peace of mind. Preoccupation with health and limited pleasure leads to a morbid and gloomy outlook. The continuation of symptoms, and in some cases, a failure to respond to treatment accentuate a pessimistic mood, leading to dysthymia (depression). Negative thoughts fuel hopelessness, intensifying a depressed mood. A future without hope results in unhappiness for the chronic, severely impaired, agoraphobic patient. Depression with suicidal thoughts and sometimes suicidal attempts can be a consequence of untreated agoraphobia. The symptoms of depression are reversed rapidly as therapy progresses and the restrictions imposed by agoraphobia are overcome.

AGORAPHOBIA AND DEPENDENCY

All of us depend upon one another for various things, and in the spirit of mutuality and helpfulness, this is healthy and appropriate behavior. Friendships thrive and love flourishes as neighbors help each other and lovers selflessly please one another. Agoraphobics, however, are crippled emotionally and, like a paralyzed person, are unilaterally dependent

77

upon others. Unlike someone with a physical handicap, agoraphobics depend upon others to fulfill irrational requests based on anxiety and a fear of having a panic attack. The mechanism is quite simple. Feeling panicky, the agoraphobic makes an irrational request. The request is granted. The anxiety goes down. In the future, this ensures that another irrational request will be made. Unhealthy dependency is the result. For example, when an agoraphobic asks to leave church prior to the completion of the service or to turn around and drive home before reaching a destination, compliance decreases anxiety but, unfortunately, increases future illogical requests. An act ordinarily thought of as a kindness actually makes the agoraphobic more dependent and psychologically weaker.

One of my patients, an agoraphobic woman, instructed her husband to call her on the telephone every half-hour when he was away from home. Another phobic woman insisted that her husband carry a beeper and install a telephone system in both of their cars. Spouses are often recruited in a conspiracy to excuse phobic behavior. One agoraphobic man who found it difficult to leave home and go to work each morning demanded that his wife call his boss and make excuses for him. Another agoraphobic man who could not take his children to a football game told his wife to explain that "daddy had the flu". Social and recreational events may be avoided with such lame excuses as one "is sick" or "has another engagement". Irrational demands by agoraphobics and over-dependency on spouses and friends severely test marriages and personal relationships.

AGORAPHOBIA AND ALCOHOL

In most civilizations, alcohol has had a prominent place during festivals and celebrations. In Greek mythology, Bacchus, the god of wine, has been associated with frivolity and good cheer. Alcohol is a socializing substance which lubricates interaction among people. Alcohol is also a tranquilizer, and many have experienced its effect of easing anxiety and lowering nervous tension.

Many agoraphobics quickly discover the tranquilizing effects of alcohol and resort to this psychoactive substance as a form of "self-treatment". Alcohol quickly ameliorates anxiety; however, the effect is short-lived and in the long run worsens agoraphobia. Studies have shown that up to 20 percent of patients with panic and agoraphobia have alcohol or drug abuse problems. Agoraphobics who choose alcohol trade temporary relief for a psychoactive substance use disorder. Agoraphobia and alcohol do not mix. If both are present, both must be treated.

QUIRKS OF AGORAPHOBICS

Over the years, I have been exposed to a number of "quirks" which are a tipoff for agoraphobia. Prospective patients may call me many times before making an appointment. They ask the same questions about panic attacks, physical illness, the use of medication, and treatment methods. The patient seeks reassurance but the manner in which questions are asked indicates a lack of trust of the professional. It

79

takes a while to realize that fear, not a challenge of the doctor's competence, motivates these repetitive questions.

Housebound patients call and ask if I make home visits. My answer is yes. Agoraphobic patients often abruptly cancel appointments, giving a wide variety of vague excuses. In reality, patients are experiencing anxiety symptoms and are fearful of coming to my office. When I look into my waiting room and see a new patient surrounded by relatives, I suspect panic disorder with agoraphobia. Many panic stricken patients are too fearful to come to my office unescorted.

Agoraphobic patients frequently fear that they will die, lose control, or go crazy. Despite repeated reassurance, agoraphobics always seem to dwell on a bad outcome. Patients frequently ask, "Are you 100 percent sure that there is nothing physically wrong with me?" Admitting to the agoraphobic that nothing in life is 100 percent and that there is a small but highly improbable possibility of physical illness, only serves to elicit a knowing smile which suggests, "See, even you, the doctor, cannot guarantee that I don't have something physically wrong with me."

Agoraphobic patients sometimes take liberty with the truth. They have a habit of rationalizing when not complying with treatment recommendations. Prevarication is not malicious, but reflects an ineffective way of coping. Agoraphobic patients are embarrassed and ashamed of their phobic behavior; rather than admit that their behavior is irrational, they have a tendency to make excuses. Successful treatment of agoraphobia requires a daily commitment to carry out homework assignments. The most common alibi for failure to follow through with recommendations is lack of time. This, of course, is a lame excuse. If patients continue to complain of symptoms and refuse to follow treatment recommendations, gentle confrontation is in order.

Feeling insecure and fearful, agoraphobic patients eagerly seek reassurance from others. Talking to other agoraphobics who are in the same predicament can lead to acceptance of the symptoms of anxiety disorder and reduce rationalization. Many of the peculiarities of agoraphobics stem from fear, bewilderment, and inadequate coping skills. Of course, successful treatment eliminates most of these quirks.

RESPONSE TO CRISIS

One would assume that the emotionally crippled agoraphobic would be unable to respond to a crisis. This is not true. It has been my experience that when agoraphobics are confronted with realistic problems, they usually muster their resources and cope very well with the crisis. For example, if the spouse of an agoraphobic gets sick and is hospitalized, the phobic reaction of avoidance frequently diminishes or may completely disappear. The agoraphobic visits the hospital, cares for the sick spouse, maintains the household, and carries on with duties that had previously been avoided because of fear.

One of my recovered patients suffered the accidental death of her only child. Although upset and grieving, she managed to cope with this tragic loss and did not experience any panic attacks. She attended the wake, the funeral, and returned to work two weeks after her son's death. She was emotionally distraught and depressed, but her symptoms of agoraphobia did not recur. Similar realistic crises such as sudden financial reversals, separation and divorce, job loss, or physical illness are faced with forbearance and fortitude by most agoraphobic patients. One explanation is that these problems are not imaginary and must be faced. Problem-solving displaces elements of phobic thinking from the mind, which in turn reduces anxiety. Unlike the "what would happen if . . . ?" thoughts which represent imaginary problems, those encountered during an emergency have to be met. As solutions emerge, the stress associated with the crisis diminishes. All too often, however, once problems have passed and things have returned to normal, the old patterns of agoraphobia — phobic thinking and the phobic reaction of avoidance — return.

Part III

The Cause of Anxiety Disorders

The Three E's

Angst, The Son of Pan

6

Other Anxiety Disorders

A brief description highlights similarities and differences among the various anxiety disorders. Each anxiety disorder is distinctive, and specific criteria separates one from the other. GAD patients are tense, high-strung, and nervous. Simple phobics usually have only one phobia which may or may not be disruptive. Social phobics have difficulty performing in public and fear criticism; timidity and shyness in social situations result from an attempt to avoid embarrassment and humiliation. Post-traumatic stress disorder, an anxiety disorder first formulated in 1980, is precipitated by a traumatic event which poses a serious threat to life or limb. There is some overlapping of symptoms among all of the anxiety disorders; hence, there is a commonality in approaches to treatment. Each anxiety disorder, however, has distinctive qualities in terms of grouping of symptoms, clinical course, specific treatment, and prognosis.

CHART 8

THE ANXIETY DISORDERS

Generalized Anxiety Disorder (Stress)
Obsessive Compulsive Disorder
Simple Phobia
Social Phobia
Post-Traumatic Stress Disorder
Panic Disorder
Agoraphobia

GENERALIZED ANXIETY DISORDER

Generalized anxiety disorder (GAD), also called chronic anxiety or stress, afflicts millions of humans. People suffering from GAD are the worriers of the world. In addition to worrying excessively, their minds are filled with all sorts of unrealistic problems. An elephantine memory dredges up old problems anew each day. Many GAD patients lament their own faults as well as complain about the inconsistencies of others.

Chronically anxious persons flock to their internist or family physician for treatment of a wide assortment of stress-related ailments. Headaches, muscle aches, peptic or gastric ulcers, and ulcerative colitis are but a few disorders which are caused or aggravated by stress. When they become symptomatic, overly anxious people are likely to respond to

television commercials, urging them to buy propri-
etary remedies. Analgesics, antacids, anti-spasmodics,
vitamins, elixirs, and related products promise release
from the stress-related symptoms. The family practitioner or internist is consulted when symptoms intensify or persist. It is safe to assume that the vast
majority of chronically anxious people ordinarily do
not seek psychiatric treatment. Psychiatrists and other
mental health professionals enter the clinical picture
only when symptoms do not respond to the ministra-
tions of the family physician.

According to the *Diagnostic and Statistical
Manual of Mental Disorders, Third Edition-Revised*
(DSM-III-R), GAD is manifested by symptoms from
the following three categories:

1. *Motor tension* — trembling, twitching, feeling
   shaky, muscle tension, aches, soreness, rest-
   lessness, and easy fatiguability
2. *Autonomic hyperactivity*— shortness of breath
   or smothering sensations, palpitations, accelerated heart rate, sweating, cold clammy hands,
   dry mouth, dizziness or light-headedness,
   nausea, diarrhea, other abdominal distress,
   flushes or chills, frequent urination, and trouble
   swallowing or "lump in the throat"
3. *Vigilance and scanning* — feeling keyed up or
   on edge, exaggerated startle response, difficulties concentrating or mind going blank
   because of anxiety, trouble falling or staying
   asleep, and irritability

DSM-III-R goes on to state that the essential
feature of this disorder is unrealistic or excessive

anxiety and worry about two or more life circumstances for six months or longer, during which the
person has been bothered by these concerns more
days than not. A realistic appraisal of the source of
worry reveals that it is usually not justified. It must
be determined that the generalized anxiety is not due
to a physical cause, e.g. caffeine intoxication, hyperthyroidism, or other conditions mentioned in Chapter 3. In GAD, worry is not related to fear of specific
objects or situations (simple or social phobia), being
contaminated (obsessive compulsive disorder), fear
of having a panic attack (panic disorder), or following a life threatening trauma (post-traumatic stress
disorder).

OBSESSIVE COMPULSIVE DISORDER

Obsessions are recurrent, persistent thoughts and
visual images that are perceived as intrusive and
senseless, but still evoke significant anxiety. At times,
obsessions seem to be demonical in origin and outside volitional control. Beset by evil spirits is the old
definition of an obsession. Indeed, this seems to be
the case when patients struggle with unreasonable
impulses which overpower their rational mind.

Obsessions generally center around three themes.
Although there is overlap of the three, one pattern
usually predominates. The three subtypes are:
1. Obsessions involving contamination, leading
    to compulsions of hand washing or cleaning,

2. Obsessions involving violence, leading to compulsions of checking, rechecking, counting, and touching,
3. Obsessions involving fear of making decisions leading to: (a) compulsions of over-meticulousness and procrastination, or (b) compulsions of hoarding.

Obsessions by definition are irrational. For instance, the idea that all germs are lethal and pose a constant threat conflicts with medical knowledge. Thoughts of deliberately harming another person are contrary to an obsessive patient's usual peaceful nature. Inordinate fear of making decisions exaggerates the consequences of most actions. Obsessions generate anxiety and this is perceived as a threat. The uneasiness or fear seems to confirm, by circular reasoning, that there is real danger associated with the obsession. Afflicted persons experience a strong impulse to rid themselves of their discomfort when anxiety reaches extremely high levels; compulsive rituals then develop as an ineffective solution to lower anxiety.

Compulsions are persistent and ritualistic motor acts or behaviors which seem irresistible and beyond control. For example, patients who are obsessed with contamination by dirt or germs feel compelled to engage in hand washing or other cleaning rituals. For those who suspect that they may have committed an act of violence, checking rituals temporarily reassure the obsessive that no violence was committed. Although compulsions allay anxiety, victims of obsessive compulsive disorder (OCD) seem either unaware of this relationship or consider it to be unimportant. OCD patients feel that they have no choice and must engage in compulsive rituals to avert a catastrophe.

OCD patients recognize that their behavior is excessive and unreasonable; however, this rational assessment does not control the compulsion. For example, when anxiety is generated by fear of contamination, the impulse to engage in compulsive cleaning rituals is overwhelming although there may be little evidence of a contaminant.

Some OCD patients are fearful that they may be responsible for a violent act, despite lack of proof. They engage in compulsive rituals of checking and rechecking to reassure themselves that violence was not committed. The compulsive checking lowers anxiety and the patient is temporarily relieved; time and energy are wasted on this pursuit and it is never completely satisfying. Other OCD patients are fearful about the consequences of their decisions, so they engage in meticulous rituals of scrupulosity and procrastination. These rituals lower anxiety and delay decision-making. Wasted time and incomplete assignments are the price paid for this compulsion. When indecision is related to discarding unneeded items, hoarding is the compulsive act. In reality, compulsive rituals are irrational, consume large amounts of time, and interfere significantly with occupational functioning, social and recreational activities, and relationships with others.

Obsessions and compulsions are inextricably linked. The anxiety-evoking obsession is always followed by the anxiety-lowering compulsion. Intellectually, the obsessive may know that most germs are harmless and do not cause disease, that violence is not in his/her nature, or that horrible consequences will not result from imperfect decisions. These rational assessments are overpowered by the irrational obsession and the anxiety-reducing capacity of the compulsive ritual.

Obsessions are comparable to phobic thinking in agoraphobia, both generate anxiety. Compulsions are analogous to phobic avoidance, both lower anxiety. Unfortunately, compulsions and phobias are reinforced by this anxiety decrement. The relationship between anxiety production and decrement is seldom understood by OCD patients.

SIMPLE PHOBIA

Many years ago when I was a student, a patient complained of a fear of 10 feet tall, orange, chartreuse, and yellow-spotted black spiders with long hairy legs and large pointed teeth. Disenchanted with the symbolic significance of this arachnid, I went to the library to investigate simple phobias. Armed with a therapeutic repertoire, I endeavored to desensitize my patient from her spider phobia. After a while and with considerable embarrassment, it dawned on me that there were no 10 foot spiders in the world, especially with the accouterments described by the patient. The giant, gaudily colored spider was but one of the many apparitions within the mind of my troubled patient. I did not know the definition of a simple phobia.

A simple phobia is a fear and avoidance of specific and discrete environmental objects or situations (not social or agoraphobic). When encountering a phobic object or situation, fear and high anxiety are experienced. As in agoraphobia, avoidance or escape from the phobic stimulus is accompanied by a subjective feeling of relief which reinforces the phobic avoidance.

Any object or situation in the environment is capable of becoming a phobic stimulus. The Anxiety Source Profile (ASP) helps identify the environmental sources of simple phobia (see Appendix). When an environmental situation produces pathologic anxiety but does not result in avoidance, the person is suffering from phobic anxiety and not a true phobia.

A simple phobia is not necessarily a disabling disorder. Some people have a simple phobia without significant impairment in any area of life. A phobic should always ask the question: "To what extent does my simple phobia interfere with my everyday living?" A decision to seek treatment depends upon the answer. For example, a fear of flying would hardly be incapacitating to a monk living in a monastery, but it could seriously hamper, both professionally and economically, a traveling salesman or a business executive.

The most common phobia is a fear of animals. A simple phobia of dogs, cats, rodents, or snakes can be annoying or terribly disabling. Unless one is a herpetologist, lives in the country, or near marshes, a phobia of snakes need not be treated. People with phobias of rats or mice might be well advised to first consult a good exterminator before seeking a therapist. A simple phobia of domestic animals, on the other hand, greatly restricts one's activities because these animals may be unexpectedly encountered anywhere.

There are many different kinds of simple phobias as can be seen from the ASP in the Appendix. It is estimated that 12 to 15 percent of the population have a phobic disorder in any six-month period. Simple phobias are not so simple. They can interfere with one's vocation, health, travel, personal relationships, and recreation. Simple phobias can become complex and incapacitating in their severe form.

SOCIAL PHOBIA

Social phobics avoid performances, e.g. public speaking, acting, engaging in sports because of an excruciating fear of criticism from spectators. Unlike simple phobics who avoid certain objects or situations, people with a social phobia avoid activities where they are required to carry out specific actions which are visible to others. Social phobics overreact to their errors and are exquisitely sensitive to disapproval, fearing embarrassment and humiliation. Prior to a performance, social phobics ruminate about possible mistakes and public ridicule. By the time of their appearance, social phobics are a nervous wreck. If possible, they avoid performing or do so with high anxiety, thus increasing the possibility of an error in their presentation.

The most common social phobia is speaking in public. Most of these phobics have a history of unpleasant or extremely embarrassing experiences while speaking. Hesitant or stammering speech, difficulties in recall, "freezing up", and similar verbal miscues in the past are indelibly etched on the mind. These recollections produce intense anxiety which leads to an avoidance of public speaking. This social phobia may not be a problem unless circumstances dictate a public speaking performance which cannot be easily avoided.

Another social phobia, found almost exclusively in males, is an inability to urinate in public lavatories. Even when the need is great and the bladder overly distended, urination is not possible in public toilets when another person is present or expected. Under these conditions, the autonomic nervous system tightens the bladder sphincter, making it impenetrable to the flow of urine. The failure to micturate in the presence of others, the social phobic believes, will lead to ridicule and result in humiliation.

Another type of social phobia involves a tremor of the hands. These phobics, when using their hands, fear that the tremor will interfere with a task. The worst case scenario includes thoughts that the tremor will spread and magnify into gross, uncontrollable movements of the body, causing people to laugh, smirk, or in some way belittle them. Eating is associated with spilling food, writing with illegibility, and both with derision. Seemingly simple tasks are approached with agony and avoided if at all possible. Striking a match to light someone's cigarette, working in front of others with one's hands (especially if the work requires fine hand movements), or signing a credit card slip are approached with extreme apprehension by the social phobic. Musicians, especially those who play instruments which require precise finger movements, may avoid playing in front of an audience. In the case of professional musicians, a social phobia may mean unemployment.

Social phobics generally evade participation in athletics, especially competitive sports. Golf swings and tennis strokes go awry when attempted with muscles tense from anxiety. Some professional athletes develop a social phobia which can seriously hamper their performance and career. One professional football player could kick long, accurate field goals at practice; however, when observed by 50,000 fans, his kicks were short and inaccurate. The author has treated professional golfers who were perfect during practice but choked during tournaments. The professional athlete with performance anxiety is faced with an excruciating dilemma — to control anxiety sufficiently to allow for maximum performance or to quit competitive sports.

Social phobics may be deprived of potentially pleasurable recreational activities such as acting in a play, singing in a choir, or playing tennis. They prefer nonparticipatory, solitary activities. Simple delights such as dancing, parlor games, or group discussions may be avoided because of fear. The vicissitudes of a social phobia may extend to any situation where social anxiety is high. Performance, whether it be trying a case in court or kicking a football, is the common denominator which causes fear. The degree of impairment is determined by the scope and frequency of avoidance behavior. In severe cases, this may encompass a wide range of social behavior.

POST-TRAUMATIC STRESS DISORDER

Post-traumatic stress disorder (PTSD), also known in the past as traumatic neurosis, is an anxiety disorder which develops after an individual has been exposed to a serious threat to life or physical integrity. The trauma that precipitates the disorder is outside the range of usual human experience and would be markedly distressing to almost anyone. A wide variety of stressors can precipitate PTSD: vehicular or industrial accidents, exposure to chemical substances (gasses, poisons), criminal or sexual assaults (rape, child abuse), exposure to disasters (earthquakes, floods), or war. The environmental trauma must involve a realistic threat to one's life or limb.

PTSD is unique from other anxiety disorders because of the following:

1. History of a specific traumatic incident during which the victim was exposed to a serious threat to life or physical integrity. The trauma may or may not be associated with physical injury.
2. Persistent ruminations about the traumatic incident and speculation about death or physical injury.
3. A repetitious reliving of the trauma in imagination (flashbacks).
4. Intense psychological distress at exposure to

events that symbolize or resemble an aspect of the traumatic event.

5. Nightmares involving the traumatic incident or a comparable situation.
6. Alterations of usual behavior following the trauma often described as a personality change.
7. A post-traumatic phobia or phobic anxiety.
8. A vengeful attitude towards individuals or groups believed to be responsible for the traumatic incident.
9. Hypersensitivity to noise usually resulting in a startle response.

Signs and symptoms often found in PTSD as well as other anxiety disorders include:

1. Generalized anxiety (nervousness).
2. Persistent physical symptoms, especially pain in the absence of objective physical findings.
3. Sleep disturbance.
4. Diminished involvement in pleasurable activities.
5. Lack of sexual desire.
6. Disinterest in family or friends, frequently leading to isolation and marital disharmony.
7. An inability to work.
8. Secondary depression, crying spells, feelings of helplessness and worthlessness.

A study of Vietnam veterans suffering from post-traumatic stress disorder disclosed that they responded with high anxiety in experiments using the drug yohimbine. According to Dr. Dennis Charney, this finding is supported by a large body of preclinical evidence relating uncontrollable stress to brain mechanisms. It may be that severe trauma to humans results in persistent brain neurophysiological dysfunction leading to the symptoms of PTSD.

In PTSD what appears to be a potpourri of symptoms is really a complex and well-organized set of pathologic behaviors, interlaced with multiple issues occurring at different periods of time. PTSD in its severest form affects almost every area of life. Beset by the multiple symptoms of PTSD, victims, in addition to experiencing anxiety, often become demoralized and depressed. Unemployment is common, especially when PTSD is accompanied by physical injury. Marital and family relationships deteriorate as PTSD sufferers withdraw into themselves. Diminished involvement in recreational and social activity hampers pleasure. Some PTSD victims become addicted to alcohol or other drugs as they self-treat their anxiety and depression. The patient's entire life seems centered around the traumatic incident.

The Environment

7

Our Surroundings and Anxiety

THE ENVIRONMENT

INTRODUCTION

When giving a lecture on anxiety disorders, I always ask the students, "What are the causes of panic and anxiety?" After they grapple with the problem for several minutes, I say unequivocally that the source for the production and maintenance of panic and anxiety must come from the environment, encephalic events (the videotapes of the mind), and endogenous processes (physiological events of the brain and body) — the Three E's. I then invite the class to dispute this statement, pointing out that if they come up with a different explanation, I shall have to rewrite the lecture and some books I have written. Thus far, no one has successfully challenged my thesis.

The first "E", environment, represents the aggregate of forces, both good and bad, which impact on us from our surroundings. The environment initiates anxiety and in many cases maintain it. Doctors C. Barr Taylor and Bruce Arnow, in their book, *The Nature and Treatment of Anxiety Disorders*, emphasize the importance of environment in the family, culture, work, and social milieu in the context of one's genetic endowment and psychological development.

In addition to the family, work situation, and social encounters, environmental sources of anxiety include a host of other situations. The ASP (see Appendix) lists common environmental sources of anxiety. A careful look at the ASP will disclose that each of the 76 items has relevance to one or more of the anxiety disorders. Filling out the form, therefore, helps to identify the environmental sources of each anxiety disorder. When the environment evokes incapacitating levels of anxiety, it is significant and requires further analysis. A review of the relationship between the anxiety disorders and the environment follows.

GENERALIZED ANXIETY DISORDER

People with GAD experience unrealistic or excessive anxiety due to worry about environmental circumstances. The environment provides the impetus for anxiety development; however, worry (encephalic activity) and concern about physical symptoms (endogenous events) sustain the disorder. GAD sufferers worry rather than sort out and address realistic problems emanating from the environment. They tend to blow problems out of proportion and inject unrealistic consequences into ordinary environmental events. GAD patients invent reasons to maintain their title: "the worriers of the world".

OBSESSIVE COMPULSIVE DISORDER

In obsessive compulsive disorder (OCD), the environment triggers obsessive thoughts. For instance, contact with a contaminant (dirt, germs, etc.) from the environment starts the cycle of obsessions which lead to compulsions of cleaning. In another subtype of OCD, environmental situations which have, in the victim's mind, potential for destructiveness, stimulate thoughts of personal responsibility for violence. This is followed by compulsive rituals of checking and rechecking. The third subtype of OCD involves an environment where decision making is required. Finalizing decisions is very painful for these obsessional persons who attribute far reaching, improbable, and disastrous consequences for an action. Personal agony becomes so intense when a decision is required that individuals delay or avoid resolving problems.

For example, a 28-year-old shipping clerk was told by his boss to solicit bids for a shipment of bananas mistakenly delivered from Central America. The clerk speculated that the bids would be well below the market price. Although the company was a large importer of bananas and could easily absorb the loss, he began to obsess about the implications of lost revenue. His company, the ship transporting the bananas, the plantation owners in Central America, and even the poor worker who picked the bananas would all suffer irreversible financial loss, he concluded. High anxiety paralyzed the clerk's action and he could not phone prospective buyers. The bananas rotted on the wharf.

Another environmental situation which is found in OCD is hoarding. Essentially, hoarding involves the inability to make a decision to discard objects which are no longer needed. For instance, an obsessive patient in tragicomic fashion insisted that his wife save for his inspection all of the garbage accumulated each day before it was to be discarded. Every evening he went through the garbage and made decisions about what would be thrown out. He rarely threw anything away and became incensed if his wife, in an attempt to instill order, got rid of garbage without his permission. Eventually, his wife threw *him* out and the marriage dissolved.

SIMPLE PHOBIAS

A glance at the ASP reveals many environmental situations which can be associated with a phobia. Being alone, journeys by airplane, elevators, pets, bridges, all can become an environmental source of anxiety leading to a simple phobia. Fear of animals is perhaps the most common of the simple phobias.

For example, a school teacher in her mid-twenties had a simple phobia of dogs which interfered with her work, causing her much misery. Many of her students brought their dogs to school each morning. Throughout the day, the dogs lounged around the perimeter of the school, frequently making a foray into the hallways. She came to work very early in the morning, parked her car as close as possible to the building, then dashed into the school to avoid any contact with a dog. She always anticipated the presence of a growling dog and was in a state of terror when it was her turn to monitor the students on the playground. Her anxiety became so intense that she quit the teaching profession.

Another patient, a widow in her late forties, was severely restricted by her simple phobia of cats. She would not leave her home unescorted because of the possibility of unexpectedly encountering a feline. Visits to friends who had cats were avoided unless preceded by a telephone call requesting that the cat be cloistered prior to her visit. Pictures of cats or their image on television would send the woman into a state of frenzy. The simple feline phobia was a major problem for this woman because it severely restricted her freedom of movement.

A phobia of storms can be particularly incapacitating, especially if that person lives in a geographic area where tornadoes and hurricanes are fairly common.

One patient with this phobia constantly monitored weather reports and darkened skies for evidence of severe storms. In New Orleans, where the patient lived, rain storms are frequent and hurricanes and occasional tornadoes are a part of the weather scene. Once, during hurricane season, the woman became so anxious and distraught that she surreptitiously packed her bags, went to the bus station, and purchased a ticket to Arizona. Before she embarked for the desert, her family intervened and insisted she seek treatment.

Some simple phobias develop in childhood. An unstable family environment and chronic anxiety do seem to have a relationship to the development of a phobia. In many cases, people adapt to their simple phobia and do not seek treatment.

For example, a young girl raised by a divorced mother of meager means always remembers being somewhat fearful of crawling insects, especially spiders. When she was 12-years- old, just prior to her mother's remarriage, she remembers running through the woods where her face and hair became tangled in a spider's web. She was terrified by the experience and became extremely phobic of spiders. Even today, at age 50, pictures of spiders send her into a panic.

Another woman from a broken home remembers that at age 4, a mouse ran into the room and her mother shrieked loudly. The mouse and the shriek frightened the young girl and she cried uncontrollably. Shortly thereafter, on her way to nursery school, she saw a dead rat in the street, cried hysterically, and had to be taken home. The woman has never required treatment, but she still has a phobia of rodents.

Although some fears may be adaptive, such as an infant's fear of strangers or a fear of heights, most phobias represent an irrational fear which is largely learned and conditioned. Traumatic incidents sometimes precipitate a phobia. An attack by a dog may result in a phobia of all canines. An automobile accident may be followed by a phobia of driving or riding in cars. The environment provides an inexhaustible source of situations which, under the proper conditions, have the potential for becoming a stimulus for a phobia.

SOCIAL PHOBIA

Performing in an environment where one is closely scrutinized stimulates high levels of anxiety in social phobics. Fear of criticism followed by acute embarrassment underlies a social phobia. Parents who are overly critical and seldom praise their progeny spawn children who are self-conscious and overly sensitive to disapproval. Being watched and evaluated while performing certain activities, e.g., speaking in public, acting in plays, or competing in athletic events, create high levels of discomfort and are avoided by the social phobic.

Social phobics are ill at ease in social environments. When a social phobic walks into a crowded room, the environment elicits thoughts that others may be critical of their dress or walk. In a restaurant, social phobics fear that their table manners will be harshly judged. While signing a hotel registry, some social phobics with a hand tremor fear reproach from the desk clerk that their handwriting is illegible. A fear of verbal miscues and being judged "stupid" inhibits the speech of some social phobics who avoid casual conversation with strangers.

Sometimes, social anxiety pervades almost every aspect of life. The following case history represents an extreme form of the disorder and illustrates the multiple environments which may be involved and avoided during the course of a social phobia.

A 36-year-old, unmarried, recently promoted clerk in a small business entered treatment with a chief complaint of fear of speaking in public. His newly acquired duties as assistant manager included a weekly meeting with his subordinates. He dreaded this assignment and could not sleep the night before the conference. Although he prepared the agenda for his talk very carefully, high anxiety interfered with an effective performance. Discovering that he disliked the meetings, his employees chided him for verbal mistakes. The assistant manager was so fearful that he might be demoted or fired due to poor performance he contemplated resigning. Outside of work, he was extremely self-conscious and inhibited; he had very limited social relationships. High social anxiety caused shyness and led to an isolated existence. Rather than mingle with people, he stayed in his apartment and watched television. When he was invited to parties he politely declined, feigning illness or concocting some other excuse. He rarely dated and had never had sexual relations with another person. His timidity and lack of social ease deprived him of many potentially pleasurable interactions with others. The young man was not schizophrenic or psychotic; his avoidance behavior was a consequence of a social phobia.

POST-TRAUMATIC STRESS DISORDER

The environment plays a crucial role in PTSD. The stressor which precipitates PTSD always originates from the environment. DSM-III-R lists a variety of stressors which can precipitate PTSD: rape, assault, military combat, natural disasters (floods, earthquakes), accidental disasters (car accidents, airplane crashes, large fires, collapse of physical structures), and deliberately caused disasters (bombings, torture, death camps).

Perhaps the most common environmental stressor which causes PTSD is a vehicular accident. Mishaps involving automobiles, trucks, airplanes, and boats can pose a serious threat to one's life or physical integrity. Another environmental source of accidents is the work place. Any place where heavy machinery may breakdown — factories, refineries, construction sites — represents a potential source of environmental trauma which may impact upon workers. Chemicals and toxic substances, whether inhaled, ingested, or absorbed through the skin, have the potential for producing physical as well as psychological pathology. An "act of God" such as earthquakes, tornadoes, hurricanes, volcanic eruptions, floods, or a bolt of lighting can cause PTSD. The carnage at the site of mass disasters can cause rescuers who handle corpses to develop PTSD.

Encephalic

8

The Mind Speaks

ENCEPHALIC ACTIVITY

As Cordes noted in 1871 among his agoraphobic patients, anxiety was based as much on ideas of the mind as it was on the environment. Encephalic activities are the thoughts and visual images commonly called "videotapes of the mind". During waking hours, all of us think or fantasize about a variety of things, such as reliving pleasant or unpleasant events from our past, anticipating success or failure regarding future endeavors, looking forward to eating a good meal, making love, seeing a hit play or movie, or enjoying conversation with a close friend. Indeed, thoughts and visual images may generate either painful emotions such as fear, depression or anger, as well as the more positive emotions of happiness and tranquility, leading to peace of mind.

Many people are unaware that they can change the way they think. Stopping or reducing unpleasant, anxiety-evoking mental activity and substituting peaceful, relaxing thoughts is therapeutic. Technically, this process is called thought stopping and thought substitution (encephalic reconditioning). There is little doubt that changing the videotapes of the mind adds a powerful dimension to the self-control of emotions and behavior.

The brain is capable of producing an endless array of verbal messages and visual images. In most anxiety disorders, the video tapes of the mind inappropriately indicate danger and are variously titled: "Accidents at Any Time," "Worry, Worry, Worry," "Terror Tomorrow," "Phobias are My Life," "Fainting and Farewell," "At the Podium," "Germs, Dread Disease and Death," and "Going Crazy." There are hundreds more of these anxiety-evoking and self-defeating "mental videotapes" with terrifying titles anticipating disaster. Panic-prone persons ponder the consequence of future actions and more often than not speculate on a bad outcome. It is important to note that the director, the producer, and the actor of these scenarios all have the same byline — the anxiety disordered person.

Depending upon the anxiety disorder, self-statements (encephalic activity) heighten anxiety. Examples include: "I am having a heart attack (panic disorder)." "I feel very nervous (GAD)." "I feel contaminated (OCD)." "That dog will jump on me and hurt me (simple phobia)." "People will laugh at me when I make a speech (social phobia)." "I could have died in the accident (PTSD)." These self-statements stimulate more alarm, more fearful thoughts, and generate more anxiety.

GENERALIZED ANXIETY DISORDER

GAD sufferers excel in worrying, an encephalic habit. As the mind whirls with unrealistic problems, excessive anxiety is produced. Worrying is second nature in GAD, and patients seem psychologically addicted to the practice. Unfortunately, they may not even be aware that troublesome thoughts excessively occupy their mind. During periods of solitude (showering in the morning, driving to work, jogging in the park, or lying in bed trying to sleep), sufferers are more likely to engage in this pernicious thinking habit. Unlike obtrusive obsessions in OCD and fearful flashbacks in PTSD, the distressing thoughts in GAD appear to the patient to be a normal mental state.

People with Type A personality have an overactive worry system which makes them vulnerable to GAD. They tend to be time urgent, irritable, impatient, self-critical, and fault finding. Type A personalities who develop GAD also think a great deal about problems they have little or no control over. An overworked encephalic system conjures up problems where no problems exist or exaggerates the significance of conflicts. Either way, distressing thoughts generate anxiety, contributing to symptoms of GAD.

OBSESSIVE COMPULSIVE DISORDER

Of all the anxiety disorders, the encephalic activity in OCD is the most intrusive. Anxiety generating thoughts seem out of control and drive OCD patients into a frenzy. Once confronted with the environmental stimuli related to contamination, violence, or decision-making, obsessions spring out like a jack-in-the-box when the lid is raised. Obsessions are inextricably linked to compulsions. In one type of OCD, uncontrollable thoughts about contamination drive victims to engage in compulsive rituals of hand washing or cleaning.

> For example, upon arising in the morning, a 47-year-old woman with a fear of dirt and germs would immediately fill her sink with water and add a powerful detergent and disinfectant. She believed almost everything in her house was contaminated. When thoughts about contamination went through her mind, she would go to the sink and dip her hands in the solution to decontaminate herself. She repeated this ritual over 300 times per day.
>
> Another patient, a 28-year-old graduate student, feared contamination from insecticides. Any contact with insecticides triggered thoughts of uncleanliness which was followed by an urgent and compelling desire to take a shower. Some days the graduate student went through this ritual five or six times. During an hour-long shower, he meticulously cleaned every part of his body.

A 37-year-old female OCD patient was somewhat embarrassed as she related the following
history. Upon accepting a package from her
mailman, her mind was filled with thoughts that
the box was covered with germs. Immediately,
she dropped the package, went to her sink, and
washed her hands with lavish amounts of soap.
Remembering that she had touched the faucet
handle when her hands were contaminated, intrusive thoughts about being unclean again
flooded her mind. For the second time she
washed her hands and also the faucet handle.
While drying her hands with the same towel that
she had used previously, thoughts about
recontamination filled her mind. She repeated
the ritual, finally drying her hands with a newly
laundered towel. Although she realized intellectually that the ritual was ridiculous, she felt
compelled to perform it.

Another subtype of OCD involves obsessions of
violence associated with the compulsion of checking
rituals. Thoughts about impulsively hurting or kill-
ing another person intrude upon the mind of these
OCD patients. Upon seeing a knife, gun, or bludgeon,
they are seized by a strong urge to use the weapon
against the nearest person. They never do, but after
the impulse passes, doubts emerge and grow into an
obsession about the possibility that they may have
injured or killed someone. When driving their car
through streets crowded with people, other OCD
patients may hear a noise and begin to speculate, and

later obsess, about the possibility of hitting a pedestrian. OCD patients might obsess about accidentally placing poison in the food of an unsuspecting person. These abhorrent thoughts of being responsible for uncontrollable and unintended acts of violence are foreign to the nature of most OCD patients.

Thoughts about violent explosions and fires can crystallize into obsessions. Objects which stimulate obsessions are: gas-operated stoves, hot water heaters, containers of gasoline or inflammable solvents, electrical switches, appliances, ashtrays containing burning cigarettes, or anything that may burn or explode. The possibility of a conflagration seems real as patients obsess about houses exploding and the incineration of loved ones. These obsessions generate intense anxiety during which the OCD patient is in a frenzied state because they irrationally assume personal responsibility for the imagined violence.

Another variation of the violence theme is fear of a criminal's forced entry into the home. These thoughts of violence are usually vague, unlike the more specific ideas of persecution in a paranoid person. Nevertheless, as OCD patients presage violation of their premises, anxiety rises and a sense of impending danger dominates their mind.

The great personal discomfort associated with obsessions of violence is alleviated, at least temporarily, when the patient engages in compulsions of checking and rechecking. Obsessed individuals who think that they have inflicted violence with a weapon may check and recheck a knife for signs of blood, a gun for evidence of recent discharge, or a bludgeon for signs of hair, flesh, or blood. Automobile drivers who believe they may have injured or killed someone retrace their route and check and recheck the scene of the supposed accident for evidence of a victim. Thinking that they may have inadvertently placed poison in the food or drink of others, some OCD patients temporarily counter apprehension by checking and rechecking the poison container to make sure that the quantity is the same as last remembered. The compulsive rituals following obsessions of fire or explosions include checking and rechecking electrical switches, gas jets, pilot lights, ashtrays, or any container of combustible materials. Window latches, door locks, burglar bars, and outdoor lights are checked and rechecked when the patient obsesses about entry into the home by an intruder. The checking and rechecking rituals rarely satisfy the insatiable appetite of the obsessive and doubts always linger.

For example, a 41-year-old police officer drove his patrol car through a crowded intersection. After passing the corner, he began to obsess that he may have hit one of the pedestrians. His anxiety rose and his discomfort became very intense. After driving ten blocks, he felt compelled to turn his car around and check the intersection. No victim was found. The officer experienced temporary relief. However, the obsession returned and he began to think about the possibility that the pedestrian was taken to a hospital. After checking several hospitals for evidence of a hit and run victim, the officer was forced to abandon his search and attend to police duties, though still feeling uneasy.

Sometimes the obsessions of violence assume bizarre proportions.

For instance, a young physician with OCD was walking down the street when he encountered an old woman going in the opposite direction. As he passed her, he had a sudden urge to smash her in the face with his fist. He struggled with this impulse and as he reached the end of the block, he wondered if he did indeed commit a felonious assault. He turned around, but she was gone. Extremely agitated, he ran down the block to check on her whereabouts, but he could not find her. Over the next several hours, he frantically phoned the police station and several hospitals to determine if an elderly lady had been a victim of assault. Over the course of the next few days, he avidly read the newspaper, including the obituaries, for reports of an assault on an old woman. He confided his fears to his wife; she reassured him that it was all his imagination, and he felt some relief. After a week, his obsession subsided but some doubt still remained.

Decision-making evokes high anxiety for many OCD patients who obsess about far-reaching, improbable, and deleterious consequences for a deliberate action. Obsessions concerning the negative effect of decision-making generate intense anxiety which paralyzes action. Personal agony becomes so great that the obsessed individual delays making a decision. Procrastination is the compulsion which pushes aside the need for action and is associated with a lowering of anxiety. Decisions are delayed or forgotten, perhaps forever.

> For example, a 28-year-old lawyer with OCD was preparing a brief. Although the attorney had all the facts and the pertinent law on his desk, he decided that more research was necessary and that more facts were needed. In reality, his inaction was procrastination or decision-avoidance due to OCD. The deadline approached and the brief was not completed. Because violation of judicial deadlines is a serious breach in legal practice, the obsessing attorney asked for a continuance of the case. This afforded immediate respite, but he continued to obsess thus delaying finalization of the brief. The attorney could not cope with his "irresistible impulse" to procrastinate and he eventually quit practicing law.

When OCD patients can no longer procrastinate and are forced to make a decision, they become panic-stricken and often make unreasonable choices. The consequence of this erratic decision-making usually leads to a bad outcome. This reinforces the conclusion that making a decision is indeed fraught with danger. Aversive experiences are incorporated into obsessional ideation related to future tasks. As anxiety mounts, the patient procrastinates, and this behavior is reinforced by the anxiety-reducing qualities of delay. This debilitating cycle increases self-doubt as decision-making is associated with great discomfort. Severe procrastinators may be fired from their job or limited in vocational advancement. They are viewed by colleagues with disdain and are frequently given unflattering descriptions such as unreliable, untrustworthy, disorganized, or lazy.

Although three distinct subgroups of OCD are described, in clinical practice one sees overlapping of these types. Usually, one type predominates in terms of symptomatic behavior. The frequency of symptoms and the degree of disability determine which subgroup of OCD is the chief complaint.

SIMPLE PHOBIA

The amount of worrying (encephalic activity) by a simple phobic depends upon how much their phobia interferes with everyday living. For example, a fear of bridges would not be incapacitating for a phobic who lives in an area where there are few bridges. On the other hand, a bridge phobic who lives in Amsterdam, New York, or New Orleans, all of which are criss-crossed by waterways, would spend considerably more time thinking about traveling over bridges. As a general rule, the greater the restriction that a simple phobia imposes upon an individual, the more time a phobic spends on fearful thinking. Those phobias which impact daily on one's life are the most severe.

A phobia of receiving injections may not concern the healthy but may be deadly for the diabetic requiring daily insulin. For one young married woman, an injection phobia interfered with her desire to bear children because she knew blood tests would be required as part of prenatal care. Thinking about his phobia of elevators led one business man to resign from his position when he was required to attend a weekly business meeting on the top floor of a high-rise building. A ship's engineer worried about his phobia of fumes from hydrocarbons and could no longer work within a ship where the smell of oil and diesel fuel was pervasive. Olfaction was also involved in the case of a young man who developed intense anxiety whenever he smelled the genital odors of a female. He avoided women sexually and for him, the simple phobia imposed celibacy. In all of these cases, thinking about the phobia occupied a great deal of time and caused considerable distress.

SOCIAL PHOBIA

Since social phobics are easily embarrassed, they worry excessively about criticism. The intensity of anxiety is proportionate to the length of time spent thinking about a scheduled social performance. When confronted with a phobic social situation, the wheels of rumination turn, stimulating anxiety. Thoughts about making mistakes in public and mental images of severe criticism from the audience flood a social phobic's mind. For example, a student who has been assigned to give a report in front of his class may think that the other students will laugh in disapproval. Oral presentations are a necessary part of education and students with this social phobia undergo considerable personal torment.

Sufferers may not seek treatment for their social phobia unless it interferes significantly with school or vocation. Worry about flunking or being fired motivates many social phobics into treatment. For example, a recently promoted executive with a phobia of speaking in public discovered that his rise in the organization included chairing a weekly meeting. Overcoming his fear of speaking in public was necessary if the young executive was to continue advancing in the corporation. A junior medical student with a similar phobia worried about presenting patients to professors and fellow students during ward rounds. The student feared failure might mean that he would not satisfactorily complete his medical studies. Sometimes circumstances dictate the necessity for treatment. A banker convicted of a white collar crime thought that his bladder might burst because of his fear of urinating in public lavatories. A federal prison lacks privacy and the socially phobic banker feared his inability to use the penitentiary's lavatories more than his confinement in prison. A businessman was transferred to the sales division of his company where he was required to write new orders in longhand. His worry about writing in front of others increased his anxiety so that his handwriting became illegible. The businessman's graphophobia led to worry about losing his job.

The encephalic habit of thinking that major mishaps will be made during public performances dominates the mind of social phobics. Memories of past errors serve to reinforce social anxiety. Worry about the reactions of others not only is related to formal presentations, but also extends to less structured activities such as talking in social situations. A large number of shy people are socially anxious and inhibited. Feeling self-conscious, they worry a great deal about the reaction of others, thus increasing their social distress, sometimes to phobic proportions.

POST-TRAUMATIC STRESS DISORDER

Reliving the trauma in imagination is a key element in PTSD. Encephalic activity (flashbacks, nightmares, and thinking about the trauma) plays a major role in the onset and development of PTSD. In fact, post-traumatic encephalic activity is the *sine qua non* of PTSD and distinguishes it from other anxiety disorders.

In PTSD, anxiety increases and is maintained by intrusive thoughts and frightening visual images related to the traumatic incident. These upsetting memories periodically erupt into consciousness and are extremely vivid and realistic. When these "video tapes of the mind" are activated by things reminiscent of the trauma, the resulting scenario retraumatizes the victim. The "mental video tapes" vividly portray the traumatic incident and may be played back in the mind several times each day for months or even years.

The fragility of life and the tenuousness of existence become dominant thoughts during the waking state as elaborations of the traumatic theme include such self-statements as, "I could have been paralyzed, blinded, maimed, or killed," and "But for the grace of God or luck or both, I should be dead."

PTSD patients tend to ruminate and speculate on the possibility that a potentially fatal consequence could have resulted from the traumatic incident. Flashbacks take on the power of an obsession, seemingly uncontrollable and very intrusive. The victim of trauma experiences flashbacks during the day and nightmares during sleep. Neither provides reassurance of survival because the scenarios always end in anxiety-evoking images depicting ongoing danger. For example, a woman who was involved in an automobile crash, which was frightening but resulted in only minor physical injuries, experienced flashbacks portraying her death, had dreams involving her funeral, and during the day thought about dying.

Encephalic activity (flashbacks, dreams, thoughts) involving various aspects of the trauma is one of the most important factors contributing to the chronicity of PTSD. Imaginal re-exposure to the traumatic event sensitizes patients to elements of the original trauma and perpetuates the maladaptive theme of future danger in the absence of any realistic threat. To a casual observer, the victim of PTSD appears to be an irritable complainer or a moody, withdrawn ruminator who is overly concerned with a trauma long past. In reality, however, the intrusive and seemingly uncontrollable mental activity related to various aspects of the traumatic experience is a key symptom of PTSD.

Endogenous

9

The Body Cries Out

ENDOGENOUS EVENTS

In anxiety disorders the brain — because of genetic factors — is extremely sensitive and, under certain conditions, suddenly produces symptoms of panic and anxiety (endogenous sensations). The victim then perceives these endogenous sensations as disruptive and dangerous. A feedback loop involving endogenous and encephalic activity occurs which further fuels the anxiety mechanism (see Figure 1). Once started, this feedback loop or "spiral effect" acts independently of any environmental event. It seems to the victim that the rapid escalation of symptoms indicates a serious physical problem.

Endogenous events play two important roles in the development of anxiety disorders. First, the brain produces the unpleasant endogenous sensations of

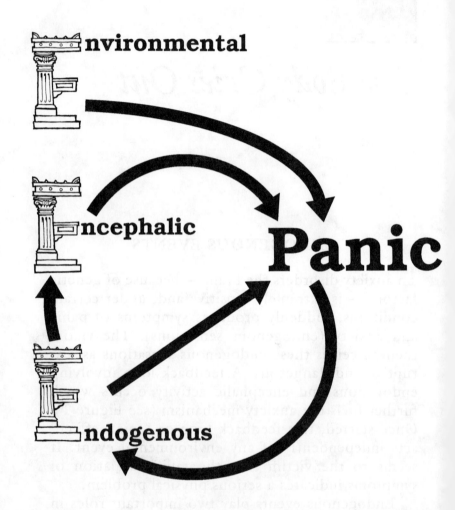

Figure 1: The Spiral Effect

panic and anxiety. Second, endogenous sensations become a source of additional anxiety when they are perceived by the brain and interpreted as hazardous. The "spiral effect" can go on and on until very high levels of panic and anxiety are reached, leaving the victim confused and scared.

A fear of anxiety symptoms and a tendency to respond anxiously to arousal has been called "anxiety sensitivity". Dr. Mark H. Pollack, assistant professor of psychiatry at Harvard Medical School, has stated, "Patients with anxiety sensitivity evidence more hypochondria and awareness of bodily sensations, lower likelihood of remission, and higher rates of phobic avoidance." Pollack points out that adult patients with a history of childhood anxiety disorders had markedly elevated levels of anxiety sensitivity. This suggests the possibility that elevated sensitivity is another manifestation of anxiety development starting in childhood and resulting in adult panic. Understanding this concept allows the patient to take therapeutic action instead of attributing symptoms to free-floating anxiety.

Among the anxiety disorders, panic disorder, obsessive compulsive disorder, and post-traumatic stress disorder seem to have the highest degree of brain reactivity, resulting in endogenously produced symptoms. Panic attacks in panic disorder, irresistible and uncontrollable impulses in OCD, and dissociative episodes (flashbacks) in PTSD seem to be correlated with altered brain activity. Spontaneous endogenous sensations play a lesser role in other anxiety disorders where anxiety seems to be largely learned and conditioned. In phobias, the endogenous effects are environmentally induced. Anxiety is produced upon confrontation or close proximity to the phobic object or situation. In GAD, environmental factors and especially encephalic activity are more important in the genesis and maintenance of anxiety.

ENDOGENOUS SENSATIONS AND MEDICATION

Evidence shows that spontaneous brain activity is responsible for endogenous sensations and that certain types of medication control anxiety-related symptoms. In panic disorder, antidepressants and benzodiazepines work directly on the brain to stop panic attacks. Obsessive compulsive behavior can be controlled by clomipramine or fluoxetine. Benzodiazepines counter generalized anxiety or anxiety associated with phobias. The fact that medications can inhibit pathologic brain activity supports the neurophysiologic mechanism in anxiety production. Medications correct biochemical deficiencies in the brain, thus diminishing endogenous sensations and symptomatic behavior.

When a person experiences a panic attack, suffers an intense desire to engage in a compulsive ritual, or has flashbacks of a traumatic event, the episodes are associated with intense anxiety. These endogenous feelings in turn are perceived by the brain as an urgent danger signal. This cognitive interpretation generates more anxiety and unless interrupted, the "spiral effect" raises anxiety to extremely high levels. When medication is prescribed to stop panic attacks, curb obsessive compulsive rituals, or reduce flash-backs, the feedback loop is broken, and correspond-ingly, anxiety diminishes. What happens is that the brain does not discharge as intensely or frequently when a patient is taking medication. The feedback loop or "spiral effect" no longer functions so there is a diminution of the cognitive interpretation of danger and no further escalation of anxiety.

As psychopharmacology becomes more sophisti-cated, medications will become symptom specific. We already see the trend with antipanic, anti-OCD, antianxiety, and antidepressant medications. It is conceivable that in the future we will have anti-worry medication, anti-phobia drugs, and more effective medications for flashbacks in PTSD.

Pan and the Trident of the Three E's

10

The Three E's and the Anxiety Disorders

The triad of the Three E's, symbolized by the trident in Pan's hands, graphically illustrates the cause of all the anxiety disorders. The interplay among the Three E's — stimuli from the external world, thoughts and visual images from the mind, and the internal physiologic processes of the brain and body — are the only sources of panic and pathologic anxiety. It follows, therefore, that the first step in the successful treatment of the anxiety disorders, including panic and agoraphobia, depends on understanding and identifying the Three E's.

PANIC AND THE THREE E'S

The concept of the Three E's presents what has been called a biopsychosocial viewpoint to explain panic and anxiety. In panic disorder, medical evidence points to a genetically determined biological component of the central nervous system which is fundamental. A complex interaction among the genes, psychological development, learning, physiology, and biochemistry produces the symptoms and behavior of panic. The concept of the Three E's embraces all of these components but condenses and simplifies the cause of panic and anxiety in a way which is useful for treatment.

ENVIRONMENT

Environmental events comprise those psychosocial factors which produce anxiety and contribute to panic. Unfavorable interaction with people usually tops the list of stressful situations. Other important sources of environmental anxiety include job dissatisfaction, financial predicaments, family frustrations, and problems of everyday living. Ordinarily, people cope with the daily pressures of life; however, in a vulnerable individual, environmental factors assume more significance and are often associated with the onset of a panic attack.

ENCEPHALIC

Prior to the development of the first panic attack, encephalic activity (worry, rumination, or troublesome thoughts) is usually above normal. After the first panic attack, the content of the videotapes of the mind then includes worry about having another attack and soundness of mind and body. As time passes, the mind of a panic attack victim becomes overloaded with scenes of imagined danger. The constant replaying of these mental videotapes portraying fearful situations abnormally increases anxiety throughout most of the day.

At night, the mental videotapes continue in the form of dreams and may be associated with insomnia and sleep panic attacks. In a study by Drs. Thomas A. Mellman and Thomas W. Uhde, it was determined that the majority of panic disorder patients in clinical treatment had experienced sleep panic. A subgroup of panic patients appear to have sleep panic as a recurrent and, in some cases, predominant symptom. Sixty-nine percent of their patients reported having sleep panic at some time in their lives, and 33 percent experienced recurrent sleep panic.

ENDOGENOUS

Endogenous sensations are central in the production of panic attacks. In the vulnerable individual, the brain is peculiarly sensitive, and under certain conditions discharges suddenly, producing the awful feeling of panic. Endogenous sensations are a two-way street. Panic and anxiety symptoms produced by the brain return through the neuro-network where they are perceived as dangerous and possibly life-threatening. A feedback loop is established between endogenous sensations and encephalic activity causing a heightening of anxiety. The victim, unaware of this "spiral effect", experiences a feeling of helplessness and loss of control as the attacks seem to occur without reason. An understanding of the concept of the Three E's allows one to pinpoint the source of panic-anxiety in order to reduce or eliminate these symptoms.

AGORAPHOBIA AND THE THREE E'S

Agoraphobia develops as a reaction to panic attacks. In an attempt to ward off symptoms, agoraphobics engage in phobic thinking and develop the phobic reaction of avoidance. Phobic thinking represents encephalic activity, and the phobic reaction of avoidance is an environmental maneuver to lower anxiety. The interplay among the Three E's produces the syndrome of agoraphobia.

ENVIRONMENT

To an agoraphobic victim, the environment serves both as a threat and asylum from panic-anxiety. The phobic reaction of avoidance provides escape from anxiety (places which have been associated with panic) and allows refuge to a safe environment, usually the home. Agoraphobics avoid certain environments because they are afraid that a panic attack might erupt in that place. Phobic avoidance allows anxiety to diminish, thus assuring an environmental mechanism which can ease discomfort.

ENCEPHALIC ACTIVITIES

Also called anticipatory anxiety, phobic thinking captures the mind of all agoraphobic victims. Prior to almost every activity, thoughts about the possibility of experiencing a panic attack run rampant through the mind. Severely impaired agoraphobics are con-sumed with catastrophic thoughts, leaving little time to think about anything else. The mind becomes over-loaded with thoughts of dread, terror, panic, alarm, and watchfulness. The agoraphobic is as much addicted to anxiety-evoking thoughts as an addict is to drugs. Doctors often have as much difficulty persuading agoraphobics to abandon their addiction to phobic thinking as they do in asking a drug addict to give up drugs.

ENDOGENOUS EVENTS

The role of endogenous events (brain activity and physiological sensations) in the production of panic attacks has been explained in the preceding section. Suffice it to repeat that without panic attacks, agora-phobia would not develop. Following a panic attack, the victim is in a state of frenzy. What to do if another panic attack strikes dominates the mind and governs future behavior. The syndrome of agoraphobia (the phobic reaction of avoidance and the self-defeating habit of phobic thinking) develops in response to panic and the threat of future attacks.

OTHER ANXIETY DISORDERS
AND THE THREE E'S

In GAD, chronic anxiety becomes part of a life style. Because nervous tension is always present, it is difficult for some patients to pinpoint the source of their anxiety. In applying the concept of the Three

139

E's, it becomes obvious that two of the E's (endo-genous and encephalic) play a major role in sustain-ing chronic anxiety. The third E (environment) is usually responsible for major fluctuations in anxiety level. The interaction among the Three E's deter-mines the intensity and duration of anxiety experi-enced by each patient. For example, a mother may be overly concerned about her son who has recently gone to college (environmental factor). She begins to worry excessively about his safety and well being (encephalic activity). The worry is unrealistic because the son is 18-years-old and has always been respon-sible. Inordinate worry begins to produce physical symptoms (endogenous sensations) which become an additional source of anxiety. Although the college student exhibits no problems and has an exemplary academic record, the mother worries throughout the school year that something might happen to her son. In GAD, the environmental source for anxiety may change (worry about finances, marriage, health, etc.), but excessive encephalic activity (worry) remains a constant. Anxiety-related symptoms (endogenous sensations) complicate the clinical picture if concern for health becomes an additional worry.

There is a definite interaction among the environ-ment, encephalic activities, and endogenous factors in the genesis and maintenance of OCD. A peculiarly sensitive nervous system and altered brain functioning (endogenous component) is probably necessary for the onset and perpetuation of the disorder. Thereafter, certain environmental cues stimulate obsessions (encephalic activity), producing high levels of pathologic anxiety. Engaging in compulsive rituals (environmental actions) serves temporarily to lower anxiety. The cycle of obsessions and compulsions whirls, often severely incapacitating the victim.

Indirect evidence of a biological factor (endogenous) in OCD evolves from the fact that certain medications disrupt the obsessive compulsive cycle in a majority of patients. In 1990, clomipramine was approved for use by the Food and Drug Administration and for the first time is available in the United States for OCD patients. Another medication, fluoxetine, has also been used successfully in the treatment of OCD.

In simple and social phobias, the environment triggers alarming thoughts (encephalic activity), which in turn produces anxiety symptoms (endogenous sensations). If contact with a phobic object or situation can be predicted, anticipatory anxiety (encephalic activity) precedes actual contact with the environmental cue. In this case, anxiety slowly builds and reaches a peak upon contact with the phobic object or situation. Anxiety (endogenous sensations) results from a combination of environmental events and encephalic activity. The interaction of the Three E's reinforces phobic behavior when it results in avoidance.

After many years of studying patients with PTSD, I have developed "The Traumatic Principle". It states, "Any environmental stimulus which poses a realistic threat to life or limb, impacting on one, or more likely a combination of the five sensory pathways to the brain, if perceived as a serious threat to one's life or physical integrity, whether it produces physical injury or not, can be regarded as a trauma and precipitate PTSD in a vulnerable individual." Clearly the central factor in the development of PTSD is exposure to an environmental trauma. Encephalic events (flashbacks, nightmares, rumination) play an important role in the sustainment of PTSD. As the trauma is replayed in the mind, imaginal retraumatization takes place, producing anxiety symptoms (endogenous sensations). The pathologic interaction of the Three E's, unless interrupted by therapy, can go on for months, even years, or perhaps a lifetime.

THE THREE E'S — A CASE HISTORY

A 32-year-old college football coach, at the end of an exciting game which his team lost in the final seconds, experienced dizziness, intense chest pain, a rapidly beating heart, and shortness of breath. His fellow coaches rushed him to a hospital where an examination revealed that everything was normal. Despite this report, the coach harbored suspicions that something was wrong with his heart. A few weeks later while exercising, he again experienced a sudden onset of pain and tightness in his chest, a pounding heart, dizziness, and difficulties in breathing. For the second time, he was rushed to the hospital with the same result — no evidence of physical illness. The attacks and medical consultations continued. At the coach's insistence, a cardiac catheterization was performed which revealed normal coronary arteries.

Told by his physicians that there was nothing wrong physically, the coach reluctantly agreed to see a psychiatrist. Family history revealed that his mother had been suffering from panic and anxiety for a long time. The coach, a tense, ambitious man, had suffered from a nervous stomach for a number of years. He was a conscientious and perfectionistic man with little tolerance for failure. His finances were a problem; he had just bought a house and was sending his two children to private school. His marriage was basically sound; however, against his wishes, his wife had recently secured a job to help pay the bills. Winning football games was not only an overriding priority for the coach, but also for the college president and the alumni. A raise in salary and the retention of his job depended upon a successful football season.

The coach was a worrier and he often thought about failure, especially the effect that a losing football season would have on his future. Although he was in good physical condition and exercised regularly, he was overly concerned about his health. The thought that he might have heart disease continued to plague him, even though his physician reassured him repeatedly that he was in splendid physical condition. He resented seeing a psychiatrist because of the inference that he was "crazy". Deep down, he still harbored suspicions that he was suffering from an undiagnosed heart ailment. The coach was experiencing anxiety from several sources.

An analysis of the Three E's revealed the following:

ENVIRONMENTAL EVENTS

1. Pressure from school officials and alumni to win football games.
2. Financial problems (house mortgage, tuition for private school for his two children, and relatively low pay as a coach).
3. Stress each week during a football game.
4. Marital tension.

ENCEPHALIC ACTIVITY

1. Worry about physical health.
2. Worry about finances.
3. Worry about winning weekly football games.
4. Worry about keeping his job.
5. Worry about having another "heart attack" (panic attack).
6. Worry about his marriage.
7. Worry about his sanity.

ENDOGENOUS EVENTS

1. Periodic panic attacks.
2. Rapid heart beat, palpitations, shortness of breath, chest pain, and tightness in the chest.
3. Nervous stomach (nausea and stomach cramping).
4. Feeling tense.

In the coach's case, the Three E's acted cumulatively to precipitate a panic attack. Environmental events were a constant and unremitting source of anxiety. His habit of worrying (encephalic activity) also increased and maintained high levels of anxiety. A family history of panic attacks in the mother suggested a predisposition for panic disorder. The endogenously produced panic attacks caused intense symptoms in the chest which were misinterpreted as a heart attack. Despite several normal physical examinations, the coach continued to obsess about his health and heart disease. The feedback loop or the "spiral effect" intensified endogenously-produced symptoms, further increasing anxiety and chest symptoms. Caught in the "spiral effect", the coach still believed that he had heart trouble. Panic attacks persisted, and he was beginning to avoid exercise and other physical activities. After his doctor's recommendation to see a psychiatrist, he also questioned his sanity.

The Three E's explain the genesis and maintenance of agoraphobia and point the way to recovery. Understanding the development of certain symptoms and behaviors is the first step towards getting well. Therapeutic interventions can, in most cases, remedy the harmful effects of panic and the pathological response of agoraphobia.

Part IV

The Cure of
Anxiety Disorders

The Trident Changes Hands

11

The Three E's and Treatment

With the power of the trident now in the hands of the victim, Pan is forced out of the clinical picture. Control switches from Pan to patient, as the triad of the Three E's exerts therapeutic influence on panic and anxiety. In the previous chapters, it was demonstrated that one or a combination of the Three E's can be anxiety generating. In this section, it will be shown that the environment, encephalic activity, and endogenous events can also be anxiety reducing. To put it another way, curing an anxiety disorder lies first in identification and elimination of the anxiety producing properties of the Three E's and second, by the implementation of antianxiety treatment techniques.

The key to overcoming panic, agoraphobia, and the other anxiety disorders is persistence. Establish-

ing and maintaining an environment which is condu-
cive to peace of mind requires planning and some
hard work. Creating an optimistic frame of mind
demands positive thinking, problem solving, and
mental effort. Likewise, relaxation training, appropriate use of medication, regular exercise, and good
nutrition keep the body fit and tranquil. The Three
E's offer a cure not only for panic, agoraphobia, and
other anxiety disorders, but also can be thought of as
a personal philosophy to cope with everyday stress.

No one is exempt from the effect of the Three E's.
All of us toil or play in the environment, think about
pleasurable or foreboding things, and experience
good or bad feelings in our body. Turning the trident
of the Three E's outward stops the self-infliction of
painful emotional wounds. In 1938, Karl Menninger
wrote a book that he titled *Man Against Himself.* The
thesis for the Three E's could be called, in a broad
humanistic sense, *Man for Himself.*

Changing the environment by eliminating stressful interaction facilitates treatment. Through the
process of education-enhanced communication,
anxiety disordered patients can gather and share
information with a spouse, relatives, friends, bosses,
and other important people in their life. Often this
reduces marital tension, occupational stress, and
conflicts with others. When an anxiety disordered
patient openly tries to improve interpersonal relationships, others are more likely to be helpful and
give emotional support which always lowers anxiety
and stress. Pleasure derived from social and recreational activities also ameliorates anxiety. Improving

one's health by changing nutritional habits and exercising regularly is good for the mind and body. Eliminating stressful conflicts with the systematic process of problem-solving reduces anxiety by adding control to one's destiny. For those suffering from agoraphobia or simple or social phobias, exposure treatment is an important environmental intervention. An analysis of environmental factors which influence emotions and behavior leads to many opportunities for a positive change.

The following environmental interventions are all therapeutically useful: education-enhanced communication, problem solving, reducing occupational stress, and increasing pleasure from social and recreational activities. Exposure treatment, another environmental intervention, is the treatment of choice for all phobics.

Encephalic interventions decrease worry in generalized anxiety disorder and reduce anticipatory anxiety in phobias and panic disorder. Obsessions in OCD and distressing thoughts in PTSD can also be controlled or minimized by techniques of thought stopping and thought substitution. Where panic is a prominent feature, the four reinforcing statements help to place the problem into perspective and direct the patient to relaxation treatment. For those phobics who are too frightened to embark on *in vivo* exposure, imaginal exposure may be a stepping stone to real life encounters. Controlling thoughts and changing the "video tapes of the mind" are crucially important in the treatment of the anxiety disorders.

Medication, an endogenous intervention, has special relevance for certain anxiety disorders. Antipanic agents have revolutionized the treatment of panic and agoraphobia. Other medications have proven to be a godsend for OCD patients. Antianxiety agents, the most prescribed pharmaceutical preparations in the world, have alleviated mental suffering and psychosomatic disorders in millions of patients. Relaxation is also useful in the treatment of panic and other anxiety disorders. Although it requires more effort and time to learn, relaxation adds a powerful dimension in coping with anxiety.

In the next three chapters, we shall examine in detail how the Three E's can work to produce a healing environment, change the video tapes of the mind and control brain activity in the treatment of the anxiety disorders.

The Environment in Treatment

12

A Healing Environment

An environment that is comfortable produces a sense of calmness and promotes healing. When the sensory organs of sight, sound, smell, taste, and touch are stimulated so that pleasure is evoked, the environment is ideal. For example, vacations may provide an opportunity to see new places, smell pleasing odors, taste fine food, and experience exotic sensual pleasure. During leisure time, responsibilities associated with stress are set aside and replaced with fun and a carefree frame of mind. Successful resorts provide social and recreational activities which soothe the mind and body. A vacation environment offers numerous opportunities for relaxation.

Vacation spots are not the only place which offer a peaceful environment. Hospitals provide harassed, over-worked executives with psychosomatic symptoms a change from a stressful work place to a therapeutic environment. Hospitalization itself often reverses stress symptoms without any active treatment. Every physician is familiar with the beneficial effects of environmental change. Recommendations to relax, take a vacation, reduce work, and engage in more pleasant recreational activities are part of a successful therapy program for stress related symptoms.

A pleasant environment chases away anxiety and facilitates a tranquil mood. For example, my office contains plants, paintings, oriental rugs, comfortable furniture, interesting artifacts, and indirect lighting. Decaffeinated coffee and herbal tea are available for me and my patients. My work environment is relaxing for me, and I hope also for my patients. In the same way, I encourage my patients to establish comfortable environments at their work and home. A dirty, messy house stirs up discontent which contributes to anxiety. It does not take a miracle to improve the quality of one's environment, only a commitment to change it. A mop and a broom eliminate dirt and grime. Prints or posters on the wall liven up a room. A radio or stereo fills a home with soothing music, while plants and well-placed lights highlight a pleasing atmosphere. A convivial environment also includes good friends, stimulating conversation, and tasty food. Sexual activity adds spice and pleasure to one's life, and few people in the throes of passion complain of anxiety. In a quiet environment, solitary activities such as reading a good book or working on a hobby produce feelings of contentment. Outside of the home, a church, a theater, or a hillside in the country may have the same refreshing effect.

There is no doubt that improvement in the quality of one's environment causes a positive change in mental attitude which in turn reduces anxiety. I have treated many patients with chronic anxiety, depression, and persistent pain and have witnessed a dramatic reduction of symptoms following a change in environment. Recreation, as the word implies, allows the body to re-create itself in a fashion which promotes well-being.

Changes in the environment also affect the other two E's. When the environment is pleasant, thoughts turn tranquil (encephalic activity), and this in turn promotes bodily sensations of relaxation (endogenous sensations). The next section answers the question, "How can one identify and apply environmental interventions in the treatment of panic, agoraphobia, and other anxiety disorders?"

SELF-EDUCATION AND ENHANCED COMMUNICATION

Fear can blind victims to facts necessary to overcome panic, agoraphobia, and other anxiety disorders. The ASP found in the Appendix, helps anxiety sufferers to pinpoint the source of their discomfort. Accurate information corrects misconceptions about the cause of anxiety, allowing the implementation of appropriate antianxiety techniques. The environment is both the source and solace for anxiety.

The process of self-education is not a one-shot matter, but continues until anxiety symptoms are no longer troublesome. Questions concerning the rationale for certain treatment techniques come up constantly and must be answered. Consultations with doctors or therapists can be helpful in clarifying issues on the cause and cure of anxiety disorders. Self-help groups are another source of information, as sufferers of anxiety disorders meet to exchange ideas which can be useful in overcoming their anxiety disorder. TERRAP (Territorial Apprehension), founded by Dr. Arthur B. Hardy, and The Phobia Society of America, founded by Dr. Robert L. DuPont, are two organizations devoted to the dissemination of information about panic and phobias (see Appendix). Public lectures and audio or video cassette tapes may also contribute to the understanding of the anxiety disorders.

Family and friends can help or hinder treatment. Some common conflicts which concern victims of panic and agoraphobia and confound relatives and friends include: concern about dying in a seemingly healthy person, fear of physical illness when physicians fail to find any evidence of disease, fear when no apparent danger exists, and most annoying, requests or demands that seem irrational. Conflicts arise because it is difficult for the unafflicted person to appreciate that willpower alone cannot control symptoms. Sufferers view this lack of understanding as criticism. Disagreements and sometimes shouting matches interfere with successful treatment.

Enhanced communication untangles misconceptions about the nature of the anxiety disorders and alleviates interpersonal conflict. Talking of existing problems must be coupled with facts about the patient's specific disorder. Communication on irrational behavior may intensify conflicts unless the discussion includes information which is based on medical and psychological truths. The following list includes facts about anxiety disorders which, when applicable, are discussed during sessions of enhanced communication.

1. Anxiety disorders are mental disorders (all anxiety disorders).
2. Panic attacks are very frightening but always pass with no permanent aftermath (panic disorder).
3. Medication prevents panic attacks, curtails rituals in obsessive compulsive disorder and lowers anxiety (panic disorder, ODC, GAD).
4. Phobias are very frightening but the fear is unjustified (agoraphobia, simple phobia, social phobia).
5. Anticipating a bad outcome to ordinary life events is a bad mental habit which increases anxiety (all anxiety disorders).
6. The phobic reaction of avoidance lowers anxiety but it is irrational and worsens all phobias (agoraphobia, simple phobia, social phobia).
7. When family or friends comply with an irrational request, in the long run this serves only to worsen the anxiety disorder (panic disorder, agoraphobia, simple phobia, social phobia, OCD).

8. Exposure treatment is the most effective way of treating all phobias (agoraphobia, simple phobia, social phobia).

9. Emotional support and empathy from family members and friends hasten recovery (all anxiety disorders).

10. Solving any problem, even though it is not directly related to the anxiety disorder, facilitates recovery (all anxiety disorders).

11. Obsessions and compulsive rituals are irrational, a waste of time and energy, and reinforce the disorder (OCD).

12. Ordinarily, people are quite forgiving when others make errors in performance (social phobia).

13. Phobic individuals imagine terrible things will happen if they confront their phobic situation or object. In reality, actual confrontation is far less anxiety-evoking and is instrumental in overcoming phobias (agoraphobia, simple phobia, social phobia).

14. Any environmentally induced accident or traumatic incident, if it poses a realistic threat to one's life or limb, can precipitate an anxiety disorder in a vulnerable individual (PTSD).

15. More often than not, agoraphobics are not housebound but do have serious restrictions in their everyday living (agoraphobia).

16. Maintaining good physical health with proper exercise and good nutrition is important during treatment (all anxiety disorders).

17. High anxiety inhibits work performance. Work itself may be a source of anxiety. Satisfaction with one's vocation is correlated with a good outcome during treatment (all anxiety disorders).

18. In general, pleasure inhibits anxiety. Involvement in pleasing social and recreational activities fosters recovery (all anxiety disorders).

19. Worrying about things outside of one's control or about unrealistic things is always self-defeating (all anxiety disorders).

20. Agoraphobia is a response to panic attacks and represents an attempt to escape from the anxiety-evoking situation to a safe haven (agoraphobia).

21. Panic disorder and OCD have a strong biological component because both can be treated successfully with medication (panic disorder, OCD).

EXPOSURE TREATMENT

Exposure treatment evolved from systematic desensitization, a method first developed by Dr. Joseph Wolpe. The principle underlying exposure treatment is simple: repeated exposure to phobic situations in graded steps (a hierarchy) lessens anxiety and eliminates the phobic reaction of avoidance. Numerous research studies have validated the effectiveness of *in vivo* exposure in the treatment of phobias. For those phobics who persist with a treatment program of exposure, the results are superb.

Developing a hierarchy is the most difficult step prior to actual exposure. Drawing upon their experience of situations they avoid, most phobics can construct a list which evokes varying degrees of anxiety. The list can be sorted and arranged in a hierarchical fashion, from low to high anxiety.

One patient, a young law student, complained of a "shy bladder". He simply could not urinate in public lavatories. He compulsively scheduled a time and place for urination and carefully controlled his consumption of liquids. Each morning before leaving home to go to the university, he completely emptied his bladder. At noon he returned home to eat lunch with his mother and to urinate. At school he avoided drinking coffee, tea, or soft drinks. When thirsty, he would rinse his mouth with water, only sipping small quantities. He rarely tarried at the law school, returning home immediately after his last class. He was extremely fearful of using public lavatories because he thought that others, noticing his problem, would laugh at him and he would feel embarrassed and humiliated. The young law student had a social phobia. The following hierarchy was constructed and utilized during exposure treatment (Chart 9).

CHART 9

TYPICAL HIERARCHY OF A SOCIAL PHOBIC PATIENT WHO AVOIDED URINATING IN PUBLIC LAVATORIES: LOW TO HIGH ANXIETY

1. Urinating at home with no one else in the house.
2. Urinating at home but with people present in the house.
3. Utilizing any small private toilet outside the home.
4. Large public lavatory, no one present, go into a stall and close door.
5. Large public lavatory, no one present, go into the stall and leave the door open.
6. Small public restroom, go into stall and close door.
7. Small public restroom, go into stall, leave door open.
8. Large public lavatory with separate urinals, people present.
9. Small restroom with separate urinals, people present.
10. Public urinal with a trough, no one present.
11. Public urinal with a trough, lots of people present.

In addition to social phobias, exposure treatment is the technique of choice for simple phobias and agoraphobia. A program of real life exposure almost always diminishes the fear associated with a phobia. A detailed account of the technique of exposure treatment is found in Chapter 16. Although simple in concept, exposure treatment requires persistence in its application in order to achieve a reversal of the phobia.

PROBLEM SOLVING

Anxiety often leads to indecision which inhibits problem solving. Many anxious people develop tunnel vision and are unable to see alternatives to their dilemma. The resolution of existing problems diminishes anxiety, making it easier to focus on treatment of the specific anxiety disorder.

Smart people seek advice from experts. Consultations widen one's choices, thus making it easier to decide upon viable solutions. Money may not be the root of all evil, but it certainly is the cause of many problems. Advice from a money management expert about budgeting, debt consolidation, or bankruptcy can lessen financial worries. Anxieties about legal difficulties can be assuaged by a competent lawyer. Sometimes just talking to a close friend clarifies issues which can lead to problem resolution and anxiety reduction. The little nagging problems which confront most people each day can usually be placed into perspective by asking the question, "What difference will this make tomorrow?" In most cases, the problem is unimportant and merely an irritation which has no long-term significance. Ultimately, one must not forget that most problems in life eventually are resolved or forgotten.

WORK — STRESSFUL OR SATISFYING?

Work occupies a major part of one's life and can be a source of stress or a rewarding activity. Strict bosses and unpleasant confrontations with fellow workers provoke stress and anxiety, contributing to the discomfort of employees suffering from panic and agoraphobia. Dissatisfaction, complicated by anxiety and poor work performance, may cause one to quit or be fired from a job. Unemployment leads to a lack of money, placing an additional burden on the anxiety disordered patient. Sorting out problems at work and resolving them are preferable to quitting or being placed in the position of being fired.

Most employers are not oblivious to the fact that contented workers are more productive than those who grouse and are under stress. An anxious employee could ask the boss' permission to restructure each day. Tedious and stressful duties can be sandwiched between more pleasant work. Arranging tasks in a different order alters the way it is perceived. When people have some control over the manner in which they work, stress is reduced and productivity is increased. Conflicts at work can be mediated if one enters into conciliation with an open frame of mind. An analysis of the work day usually reveals opportunities for the inclusion of activities which reduce stress and make work more pleasurable. In many cases, once the anxiety disorder has been resolved, work can again be a rewarding activity.

SOCIAL-RECREATIONAL ACTIVITIES

When anxiety is high and constant, it is difficult to enjoy life. Pleasure takes a back seat to anxiety as fear overrules the desire to mix with people or to attend recreational events. When anxiety recedes, physical symptoms and phobic behavior diminish and are no longer an impediment to enjoyment. Less time is spent presaging panic, anticipating anxiety, avoiding situations, and visiting doctors. Freed from the restrictions of panic and anxiety, most patients are exhilarated by recovery. They find no difficulty with their new-found freedom. For some, however, filling the void resulting from improvement may present an unexpected problem. Those with long-standing panic and agoraphobia, for example, may be hesitant to test their wings. They need encouragement to rediscover old pleasures and to plan new ones. Once anxiety patients receive pleasure from engaging in social and recreational activities, they realize it is one of the payoffs for getting well. The environment offers many opportunities for enjoyment, and the satisfaction derived from social and recreational activities sustains improvement.

SUMMARY

In addition to self-education, enhanced communication and exposure treatment, any environmental intervention which reduces anxiety and improves the quality of life is beneficial in the treatment of anxiety disorders. Deriving more satisfaction at work, enjoying social and recreational activities, successfully solving problems of daily living, engaging in regular exercise, and maintaining good nutritional habits contribute to mental and physical well-being. These environmental interventions not only lower anxiety, but also build self-esteem and a sense of mastery.

Positive Thoughts, Emotions, and Peace of Mind

13

Changing the Videotapes of the Mind

Almost all anxious people have vivid imaginations and think too much about frightening things. Thoughts generate emotions, and bad thoughts produce bad feelings. Following a panic attack, the "videotapes of the mind" portray fearful scenes. Even if panic attacks do not occur frequently, thoughts still revolve around the central theme of danger to self. This produces anxiety which governs future behavior. The thought-feeling-behavior sequence goes something like this: thoughts about danger to self - generate feelings of anxiety — which in turn leads to self-defeating behavior, e.g., phobic avoidance. In a sense, the mental videotapes of anxious people are out of kilter. The brain, like a mis-programmed computer, is putting out the wrong information.

To a large extent, thoughts are under conscious control. Switching thoughts from bad to good changes the feeling state of the body which influences behavior. Dr. Aaron T. Beck popularized this concept and today it is known as cognitive therapy. Before cognitive therapy (encephalic reconditioning) can take place, thoughts must be identified and inventoried. Thinking is a habit and through introspection everyone can assess their encephalic activity. Thoughts can be monitored while driving to work, waiting for someone, exercising, and especially prior to sleep. Once anxiety-evoking thoughts have been identified, the erroneous "video tapes of the mind" must be erased. In a sense, encephalic reconditioning is a reprogramming of the brain. Although simple, it does require mental work and perseverance. Never forget the principle underlying this therapeutic technique: thoughts lead to feelings, and feelings influence behavior.

ENCEPHALIC INTERVENTIONS

THOUGHT STOPPING

The behavioral technique of thought stopping was first described by J. A. Bain in 1928. When anxiety-evoking thoughts are noted, the patient is instructed to shout silently but emphatically the demand, "Stop! Get out of there!" or "Stop the action!" This forceful self-statement is repeated as often as necessary to eliminate anxiety-generating thoughts. M. J. Mahoney, in 1971, suggested that a rubber band can be worn around the wrist and snapped simultaneously with the silently shouted phrase, "Stop! Get out of there!" The momentary pain and the emphatic statement effectively stop unwanted mental activity. Most people are surprised and pleased with the results.

THOUGHT SUBSTITUTION

Next, the technique of thought substitution is employed to supplant phobic thinking. Optimistic thoughts and "new videotapes of the mind" are created which evoke pleasant and relaxing feelings. The title of these new mental videotapes might be based on the theme, "What if everything turns out all right?" These new videotapes of the mind can be created from fantasy, past pleasant memories, or the anticipation of future happy events. The new scenarios are practiced several times a day or whenever the old anxiety-generating thoughts enter the mind.

THE FOUR POSITIVE REINFORCING STATEMENTS

Correcting erroneous thoughts about danger to self and the fear of physical disease can be achieved by employing the "four positive reinforcing statements". This form of encephalic reconditioning is especially useful when one begins to experience uncomfortable feelings suggestive of a panic attack. Upon noticing any bodily sensations which might be misinterpreted, victims are instructed to say to themselves:

1. *I feel uncomfortable.* (This confirms that the feelings are not imaginary and acknowledges the presence of panic-anxiety symptoms.)

171

2. *I have had these feelings before and THEY ALWAYS PASS.* (This is a true statement. No dire or irreversible consequences have ever resulted from these feelings.)
3. *There is nothing seriously* (physically) *wrong with me.* (This is also a true statement. Physical examinations and various tests have all been normal.)
4. *I am experiencing panic-anxiety.* (This is a correct assessment.) *I shall employ techniques of thought stopping, thought substitution, and relaxation and these uncomfortable feelings will pass more quickly.*

The four positive reinforcing statements are all true. As these statements are recited, the panic-anxiety symptoms will pass, especially when combined with deep breathing exercises and progressive muscle relaxation.

IMAGINAL EXPOSURE (DESENSITIZATION)

Some phobics may be too fearful to embark upon a real life exposure program. Imaginal exposure bridges the gap from fearful avoidance to successful confrontation in real life, utilizing the power of the imagination to heal. Studies have shown that imaginal exposure has nearly a 90 percent success rate in the treatment of anxiety and phobias, including agoraphobia. A hierarchy of situations is developed and imaginal desensitization begins with the lowest anxiety-evoking item. A phobic is asked to visualize that item repeatedly, alternating each scene with relaxation. When the phobic scene can be visualized without any appreciable anxiety, the next anxiety-evoking scene is introduced. Imaginal exposure is based on the principle that gradual exposure in the mind to a phobic or anxiety-evoking situation deconditions anxiety. After visualizing all items of the hierarchy, the gains achieved with imaginal exposure transfer to the real life phobic situation. The technique of imaginal desensitization has been universally applauded and will be discussed in more detail in Chapter 16.

Controlling Brain Activity:
Endogenous Events and Emotions

14

Controlling Brain Activity

ENDOGENOUS INTERVENTIONS

Controlling brain activity may seem like an awesome task, but we do it everyday. Thinking, like walking and talking, is the result of brain activity, and to a large extent, all three are under conscious control. Emotions, because of their ubiquitous nature, may seem uncontrollable; however, anxiety, depression, and their opposites, relaxation and euphoria, are related to the way we think. Thoughts can also be influenced by medication and other chemical substances. Panic attacks, obsessive compulsive rituals, and flashbacks all have roots in the biochemistry of the brain and can be affected by specific biological and psychological interventions.

175

During a panic attack, brain activity bursts upon an individual in the form of acute symptoms (endogenous sensations). The internal organs of the body are speeded up and the resulting emotions of panic and anxiety frighten the afflicted individual. In a panic attack, the brain plays two important roles. First, it produces the symptoms we call panic and anxiety. Second, once produced, the symptoms are perceived by the brain and cognitively appraised as dangerous or life-threatening. Unless interrupted, endogenous and encephalic events can escalate anxiety to a high level (see Figure 1, Chapter 9).

The feeling state of fear which occurs during a panic attack can be controlled by utilizing medication and relaxation treatment. The use of medication in panic disorder controls brain activity, stops panic attacks, and reduces anxiety. Relaxation treatment influences brain activity by reversing the feelings of anxiety and promoting calmness and well-being. Medication and relaxation are two endogenous methods which directly affect brain activity and play an important role in treatment.

MEDICATION

HISTORICAL ASPECTS

Since the dawn of civilization, humankind has searched for drugs which make a person feel good. Narcotics (substances usually extracted from plants such as opium, hashish and cocaine) are probably the world's oldest tranquilizer, but alcohol cannot be too far behind. Many have found their way into the medical pharmacopoeia and are used as analgesics and sedatives.

Although alcohol has been used over the millennia by virtually all societies, problems of abuse and dependence make alcohol an unsatisfactory antianxiety agent. In the early part of the twentieth century, concoctions containing bromide were found to have a tranquilizing effect on patients. Ethel Barrymore, of the famous Barrymore thespian family, alarmed her brothers when she appeared to be intoxicated while performing in a play. Finding no alcohol, the brothers searched her luggage and found several bottles of an elixir containing bromide. Ms. Barrymore was suffering from "bromism", an abnormal mental state due to excessive or prolonged use of bromides. She later was detoxified and went on to a brilliant career in acting.

Barbiturates replaced bromides as an antianxiety agent and sedative. At one time, barbiturates were the most widely prescribed medication in the world. For many years physicians prescribed barbiturates for various anxiety symptoms and for insomnia, as well as epilepsy. With the passage of time, it became evident that the barbiturates were extremely addicting. Users developed tolerance to the drug and abrupt withdrawal of barbiturates frequently led to convulsions. Today, barbiturates have limited use in medicine and psychiatrists do not prescribe them for anxiety disorders.

A new era in the treatment of anxiety disorders was ushered in with the introduction of the meprobamates in the 1950's. These antianxiety drugs, under the trade names of Equanil and Miltown, were originally thought of as miracle drugs for nervous tension. With experience, however, it was discovered that meprobamates, like the barbiturates, had addictive qualities. Although meprobamates are still on the market, few physicians prescribe this group of drugs for anxiety.

BENZODIAZEPINES

A breakthrough in the psychopharmacology of anxiety occurred in 1960 with the introduction of chlordiazepoxide (Librium) and a year later with diazepam (Valium). These two benzodiazepines have a remarkable record over the past thirty years for safety, therapeutic effectiveness, and toleration by patients. If taken as prescribed, the benzodiazepines have few side effects and a wide margin of safety. Over the past three decades, the benzodiazepines have been the mainstay in the treatment of anxiety and anxiety related disorders. Family physicians and internists depend upon the benzodiazepines to help their nervous patients. It is difficult to estimate the amount of human suffering which has been alleviated by the benzodiazepines.

Dr. David V. Sheehan, professor of psychiatry at the University of South Florida, was the first researcher to demonstrate that alprazolam (Xanax) prescribed in higher than average dosages was a very effective antipanic medication. Alprazolam is well tolerated by the patient, works quickly, and controls or stops panic attacks in a majority of cases. Clonazepam (Klonipin), originally prescribed as an anticonvulsant medication, has also been used successfully in the treatment of panic disorder. Clonazepam is a long acting benzodiazepine and only needs to be prescribed twice daily. Although not officially approved by the Food and Drug Administration, clonazepam is effective in clinical trials with patients suffering from panic disorder.

CHART 10

THE BENZODIAZEPINES

Generic	Brand Name
alprazolam	Xanax
clonazepam	Klonopin
lorazepam	Ativan

There are a number of benzodiazepines which have antipanic effects if used in high enough dosages. Alprazolam has been used more extensively in treating panic disorder than any of the others. Clonazepam is a long acting benzodiazepine which is being used more frequently as an antipanic agent. Lorazepam has also been studied and found to be effective in treating panic disorder. Most researchers believe that all benzodiazepines have antipanic properties, but sufficient clinical studies are lacking.

In the past, physicians hesitated to prescribe benzodiazepines in dosages high enough to block panic attack, and this retarded effective treatment for panic disorder. Another factor which prevented effective treatment was a bias among many physicians that benzodiazepines could not be prescribed for more than a few weeks. Studies originally done by Dr. Sheehan, who at the time was an assistant professor at Harvard Medical School, shattered these myths. Utilizing dosages of alprazolam twice as high as recommended by the PDR, Sheehan demonstrated excellent results with panic patients. Many of his patients were maintained on alprazolam for several months before withdrawal was attempted. If withdrawal is not successful, patients can be switched to other antipanic medications to prevent a relapse. Sheehan, in his book *The Anxiety Disease*, states, "Alprazolam is the most rapidly effective of the antipanic drugs, and the least disruptive and the least toxic to the patient. For all these reasons, it appears to be the safest to use, and it is the easiest for the physician to prescribe, regulate, and monitor."

A question that must be answered for each individual is: "How long must a panic disorder patient be maintained on benzodiazepine or, for that matter, any other antipanic medication?" After panic attacks have ceased, phobic behavior resolved, and phobic thinking lessened, the benzodiazepines can be slowly withdrawn. The response of each patient to discontinuation of benzodiazepines determines further therapy. Studies have shown that the fear of escalating the doses of benzodiazepines is unfounded. Over time, benzodiazepines can be reduced without diminishing drug efficacy. Nagy and her colleagues at Yale University have followed 60 patients for up to four years and found that the average dose of benzodiazepine (alprazolam) had decreased significantly without sacrificing therapeutic effectiveness.

THE ANTIDEPRESSANTS

Dr. Donald F. Klein and his associates discovered the effectiveness of imipramine (Tofranil) as an antipanic agent in the early 1960's. Since that time, imipramine, a tricyclic antidepressant (TCA), has been used extensively in the treatment of panic disorder and has become a standard. Although a proven antipanic medication, imipramine and many related antidepressants (see Chart 11) have unpleasant side effects which decrease patient compliance. If the patient can be persuaded to stick with a TCA for several weeks, the unpleasant side effects usually dis-

---

CHART 11

ANTIDEPRESSANTS WITH ANTIPANIC PROPERTIES

TRICYCLIC ANTIDEPRESSANTS

Generic Name	Brand Name
amitriptyline	Elavil
amoxapine	Asendin
desipramine	Norpramin
doxepin	Sinequan
imipramine	Tofranil
nortriptyline	Pamelor

OTHER ANTIDEPRESSANTS

clomipramine	Anafranil
fluoxetine	Prozac
trazodone	Desyrel

appear, while the therapeutic effects of the medication reach a maximum level. All TCA's have not been used in the treatment of panic disorder, but most clinicians and researchers believe these related medications would have similar therapeutic effects.

CHART 12

ANTIPANIC MONOAMINE OXIDASE INHIBITORS (MAOI's)

Generic	Brand Names
phenelzine	Nardil
tranylcypromine	Parnate
isocarboxazid	Marplan

Another group of antidepressants, the monoamine oxidase inhibitors (MAOI's) are also useful in treating panic disorder. Some clinicians feel that the MAOI's are superior to the TCA's or benzodiazepines; however, most clinical studies show that all three groups of medication have comparable therapeutic efficacy. The MAOI's have the disadvantage in that certain food stuffs must be eliminated from the diet in order to prevent a "hypertensive crisis". Panic patients, already tense from the dread of having a panic attack, become extremely fearful when told of a possible drug reaction. Patients, therefore, may be reluctant to take the MAOI's. If patients can be persuaded to avoid certain foods and remain on MAOI's, the results are usually excellent in controlling and stopping panic attacks (see Chapter 15).

Research indicates that two new antidepressants, fluoxetine and clomipramine, are very effective in treating obsessive compulsive patients. Clomipramine, which has been used for years in Europe and South America, recently has been available in the United States for treating OCD. Used in conjunction with specific behavior therapy techniques, OCD patients can enjoy relief from extremely incapacitating symptoms. Preliminary reports disclose that clomipramine and fluoxetine also have usefulness in the treatment of panic disorder. It is interesting to note that clomipramine has the same chemical formula as imipramine, except one chlorine atom has been added to its chemical structure.

THE BETA BLOCKERS

The beta blockers (Chart 13) are prescribed extensively in medicine to treat cardiovascular problems including high blood pressure and stress-induced angina. In psychiatry, beta blockers are used in the treatment of generalized anxiety disorder, panic disorder, and social phobia. In the treatment of GAD and panic disorder, other medications are more effective. There have been numerous reports indicating that propranolol and other beta blockers are helpful in the treatment of social phobia. Prior to a performance (public speaking, playing a musical instrument) social phobics seem to benefit from beta blockers. For individuals suffering from a social phobia, a combination of medication (beta blockers or benzodiazepines) and behavior therapy seems to yield the best results.

CHART 13

THE BETA BLOCKERS

Generic	Brand Name
propranolol	Inderal
atenolol	Tenormin
metoprolol	Lopressor
nadolol	Corgard

RELAXATION TREATMENT

One of the key symptoms of anxiety is motor tension — tightness of the voluntary muscles of the body. Headache, backache, and chest pain result when muscles remain tense for a long period of time due to chronic anxiety. Symptoms of increased muscular tension can be alleviated by employing techniques of relaxation. As one learns to relax, the various muscles of the body return to normal and symptoms of anxiety diminish. The "keyed up, edgy feeling" of chronic anxiety is soon replaced by peace of mind.

Early civilizations somehow learned of the relationship between muscle relaxation and peace of mind. Writings from the ancient Egyptians, Greeks, Romans, Druids, and even witch doctors in primitive cultures have incorporated hypnotic-like methods of relaxation in their ceremonies. Worries are exorcised from the mind with meditation and prayer. The concept that the mind can be used to relax the body has a long history which has usefulness to the present day.

During modern times, Dr. Edmund Jacobson, an internist, rediscovered the principle that relaxation of the muscles produced a calming effect on the various organ systems of the body. Jacobson applied this technique to a wide range of medical problems which were psychosomatic in origin. Published in 1938, his book *Progressive Muscle Relaxation* documents good results with patients. Over the past 50 years Jacobson's technique of progressive muscle relaxation (PMR) has been widely accepted and forms the basis for most of the relaxation procedures in existence today.

Jacobson's method of PMR consists of systematically contracting then relaxing various muscle groups of the body. As the muscles lose their tension and become relaxed, other organ systems associated with anxiety return to normal. The heart slows, breathing becomes regular, abdominal cramping disappears, moist palms turn dry, and there is a general feeling of well-being leading to peace of mind. Relaxation is the opposite of anxiety, and it is impossible for both feelings to exist at the same time. The technique of PMR is described in detail in Chapter 15.

THE THREE E'S AND THE TREATMENT OF THE FOOTBALL COACH

The football coach mentioned in Chapter 10 was treated by utilizing the concept of the Three E's. After the history had been obtained, the first meeting consisted of a conference with the coach and his wife. During this education and enhanced communication session, facts about panic and agoraphobia were discussed. Since the coach's physical health was a main issue, medical reports were reviewed and explained to the couple. Subsequent sessions dealt with the couple's financial problems and marital conflicts concerning the wife's employment. The wife was reassured that her husband was not crazy, but was suffering from an anxiety disorder. As treatment progressed, the process of education and enhanced communication continued and marital tension diminished.

The coach's attitude towards winning football games was evaluated. His desire to please college administrators and alumni was placed into perspective. Winning was important, but a philosophical approach about the outcome seemed advisable. After his team was properly prepared, a post-game analysis of their performance was a better alternative than worrying about the uncertainties of winning.

Next, exposure treatment, an environmental intervention, was employed. The coach, though not typically agoraphobic, was beginning to avoid exercise and other physical activities because he misinterpreted the normal effects of exercise as an indication of heart disease. As part of exposure treatment, the coach was encouraged to exercise regularly. Whenever he became distressed about changes in heart beat and respiration, he was to stop, wait for his vital signs to return to normal, then continue exercising. The coach gradually became desensitized to the fear associated with the physiological sensations of exercise and excitement which he formerly and incorrectly attributed to heart disease.

The coach was an Olympic class worrier and he was addicted to phobic thinking. To reverse this bad thinking habit, he was encouraged to repeat the four positive reinforcing statements when he noticed sensations in his chest which he attributed to heart disease. Nonproductive, anxiety-evoking thoughts related to winning games, finances, and marital problems were counteracted by employing thought stopping and thought substitution. It was suggested that he visualize scenarios where "everything turned out all right". He was familiar with the principle of positive thinking and readily accepted this recommendation. The coach was reassured that although he did have panic and agoraphobia, he had no need to fear for his sanity.

Antipanic medication stopped the coach's panic attacks. When he experienced mild to moderate symptoms of tightness or pain in his chest, he was encouraged to utilize PMR, especially deep breathing exercises. This endogenous intervention was combined with the four positive reinforcing statements to break up his habit of phobic thinking.

The coach was not easily dissuaded from the idea that he had heart disease. However, the prescription of antipanic medication stopped his panic attacks, making him more amenable to a psychological explanation of his remaining symptoms. Changing the videotapes of his mind and employing PMR reduced his anxiety. His confidence grew as did his acceptance of the fact that he was physically healthy, and he resumed regular activities. Enhanced communication dissipated marital tension and led to more harmonious interaction with his wife. Instead of thinking that he had to win games, the coach's attitude changed. He would do everything within his power to properly prepare his players. Afterwards, he would analyze the game and accept the outcome. Interestingly, after treatment, his team had a successful football season. Antipanic medication was eventually discontinued. The coach recovered from panic and agoraphobia.

SUMMARY

Overcoming panic, agoraphobia, and other anxiety disorders includes the systematic application of specific therapeutic interventions involving the Three E's. The Three E's act in conjunction with one another. Changes in one E produce changes in the other two. When the environment is peaceful, thoughts and visual images are pleasing, and this in turn produces relaxed feelings within the body.

Environmental interventions are: self-education, enhanced communication, exposure treatment, analysis of work behavior, and improved social and recreational activities. In addition, regular exercise and good nutrition contribute to physical and mental health. Encephalic interventions include: thought stopping, thought substitution, the four positive reinforcing statements, and in some cases, imaginal exposure. Finally, panic attacks and high anxiety can be reduced or eliminated with the use of antipanic and antianxiety medication. Any remaining symptoms can be managed by relaxation treatment. These therapeutic techniques form the basis for overcoming anxiety disorders.

Part V

Panic No More

Controlling Pan

15

Treatment of Panic

Rendered inert by the powerful effects of medication and meditation, Pan stares vacantly with unseeing eyes. No longer a menace, Pan has been tamed with antipanic medication and relaxation. The panic victim, now in a state of repose, does not recall the old thought that went through his mind each morning, "Will I have a visit from Pan today?" Now, with panic under control, the meditator muses, "I wish that this feeling would last forever." This wish is not a pipe dream because it can be granted by the stroke of a pen on a prescription pad and an audio cassette guiding the patient in the techniques of progressive muscle relaxation.

From a physician's standpoint, diagnosis of panic disorder is good news because it can be treated successfully and fairly quickly with medication and relaxation treatment. For those symptomatic panic patients who are skeptical, the diagnosis may not seem so salutary, especially if previous treatment has failed. This chapter attempts to unravel misconceptions about treatment of panic and present the methods and means for cure.

MEDICATION

There is no doubt that medication should be prescribed in panic disorder. When panic attacks erupt frequently and interfere with daily living, the data clearly indicates that the use of one of the antipanic medications is warranted. Why then do some patients refuse to take medication? Why do some therapists hesitate to prescribe or recommend antipanic medication?

THE PATIENT'S PERSPECTIVE

No one likes to take medicine. In olden days, pharmaceuticals were usually bitter and the bad taste was often concealed by a cachet, a flour-paste casing within which unpleasant tasting medication was placed. Because only rich people could afford a cachet, the word thereafter became associated with something of prestige. Nowadays, medication is usually tasteless, and an aversion to taking prescribed drugs is based on fear. Panic-prone patients are sensitive to any change produced by drugs. They frequently misinterpret side effects caused by medication as an indication of an impending panic attack.

All panic attack victims excessively monitor bodily sensations. Extreme watchfulness backfires as a warning mechanism for the onset of a panic attack.

Hypervigilance offers no protection from panic because the perception of any new physical sensation stimulates fearful thoughts about impending panic, thus increasing anxiety. Many medications produce some side effects which frighten anxious patients who wrongfully conclude that panic is pending. Even mild, innocuous side effects of medication can trigger thoughts of a panic attack. After experiencing several such episodes, some patients develop a fear or phobia of taking medicine. If the panic patient is hypochondriacal and fearful of developing some awful disease, the scenario is different but the results are the same. In these cases, the fear is centered around the idea that medication will in some way cause bodily harm, even death. Fear that drugs will cause illness can coalesce into a phobia of taking any medication.

Anyone who takes medication must be educated about side effects. If this is not done, the first episode of even minor side effects will complicate treatment. For those patients who have a phobia of medication, a program of desensitization can eliminate this irrational fear. First, a hierarchy is developed. Desensitization begins with a very small dose of medication which will not produce any noticeable side effects. As anxiety about taking medication decreases, the dosage of medication is slowly increased. Fears about medication are dissolved by the process of desensitization and the pharmacologic effect of the antipanic medication. With time, patients stop searching for the bodily sensations which arouse anxiety and instead focus their attention on overcoming panic.

Generally, patients who are phobic of taking medication will seek out those programs for panic and agoraphobia which offer help without drugs. Prior to the development of pharmaceutical agents, I successfully treated patients with panic and agoraphobia without using any medication. Today, I would not subject any of my panic disorder patients to treatment without antipanic medication. The cost in suffering, time, effort, and money is simply not worth it. Also, patients who continue to experience panic attacks during treatment become dispirited and lose confidence in therapy.

THE DOCTOR'S ATTITUDE

Most people harbor biases and professional people are no exception. Medical doctors who prescribe drugs usually favor the use of medication in the treatment of panic disorder. There is no doubt that medication stops panic attacks, and this statement is supported by numerous scientific studies. For some patients, medication may be all that is needed to stop panic attacks, diminish anticipatory anxiety, and eliminate phobias. In most cases, psychological interventions are an adjunct to the use of medication.

An opposite point of view is held by some therapists who do not have a Doctor of Medicine degree. These professionals cannot prescribe medication; therefore, they tend to favor non-medicinal treatment. In fact, psychologists and other therapists have been in the forefront of innovative psychological approaches for panic and agoraphobia. Certain behavior therapy techniques such as cognitive therapy, relaxation, and exposure treatment have proven very effective, especially in the treatment of anticipatory anxiety and agoraphobia. This bias against medication has caused some clinicians to de-emphasize the beneficial effects of antipanic agents. One need not toss out the baby with the bath water. Dr. David H. Barlow, professor of psychology at the University of Albany, State University of New York, has noted that there is significant evidence that effective psychotherapy causes change in the chemical systems of the brain, while medication results in change in the cognitive processes and other psychological aspects of panic disorder. Both medication and cognitive-behavioral techniques form the basis of a comprehensive treatment program. One should beware of therapists who exalt one approach exclusively over the other.

THE DECISION TO TAKE MEDICATION

When panic attacks occur frequently and interfere markedly with a person's life, the decision to take medication can be made without hesitation. Panic attacks foster phobic thinking and phobic behavior. When panic attacks stop, the urge to think and act phobically diminishes. If the symptoms of agoraphobia persist after panic attacks cease, psychological interventions such as exposure treatment, thought substitution, and thought stopping are easier to implement. Some patients feel a sense of personal failure when medication is prescribed. For those patients, depending on a pill collides with an independent temperament. This attitude is self-defeating. I tell my patients that they get no medals for not using medication. Medals are awarded for improvement. A panic-free, non-phobic life style is the goal, and when attained, does deserve commendation. Whether one reaches that goal with or without medication matters little.

ANTIPANIC MEDICATIONS

Antidepressants (the tricyclics, monoamine oxidase inhibitors), and antianxiety agents (the benzodiazepines) are the classes of medication which have been used successfully to treat panic disorder. The dosage of each medication is tailor-made and increased until the patient reports no more panic attacks. As will be discussed, all antipanic medications have advantages and disadvantages. The response of the patient depends upon their toleration to a therapeutic dosage. In most cases, when the proper dose of medication is reached, panic attacks stop.

TRICYCLIC ANTIDEPRESSANTS (TCA's)

Imipramine was the first medication used to treat panic attacks. It has a long history of success and many clinical studies attest to its effectiveness. Between 70 to 90 percent of patients who take therapeutic doses of imipramine experience significant symptomatic improvement. Imipramine is also available in generic form and is less expensive than other antipanic agents.

Imipramine does have some disadvantages — delay of action and unpleasant side effects. It usually takes two or more weeks to build up an antipanic dosage in the bloodstream. Unpleasant side effects such as drowsiness, rash/itching, dry mouth, constipation, delayed urination, fast heart beat, changes in blood pressure (especially if one stands too quickly), insomnia, weight gain, seizures, and sexual dysfunction have been reported. Occasionally, patients complain of "the jitteriness syndrome" (agitation, sweating, anxiety symptoms, and jumpiness). High doses of imipramine are more likely to produce side effects. "The jitteriness syndrome" and other side effects are usually short lived, reversible, and can be minimized if the starting dose of the TCA is low and gradually adjusted upward. If patients mistakenly interpret side effects as the beginning of a panic attack and discontinue the medication before the optimal dose is reached in the bloodstream, a different antipanic medication must be selected. Fortunately, most patients adapt to side effects within a very short period of time and experience the therapeutic benefit of imipramine.

Depression is often associated with panic disorder. The use of an antidepressant with antipanic properties, therefore, serves two purposes: to stop panic attacks and to alleviate depression. If anxiety remains high, it may be necessary to prescribe a low dose of one of the benzodiazepines together with a TCA. When patients learn non-medicinal anxiety control (relaxation and encephalic reconditioning), the slow withdrawal of benzodiazepines can be accomplished without difficulty.

Monoamine Oxidase Inhibitors (MAOI's)

Phenelzine is the most commonly prescribed MAOI for the treatment of panic disorder. Some investigators have reported that in the case of panic-related disorders (including agoraphobia), phenelzine is remarkably effective and might have a superiority over the TCA's. In addition, MAOI's are also helpful in the treatment of panic-anxiety and what has been called the "polysymptomatic anxiety syndrome". The MAOI's, although powerful as an antipanic agent, have some disadvantages. MAOI's have side effects similar to those found in the TCA's, which may be bothersome, but usually diminish or disappear after a few weeks. More serious is an alteration in blood pressure. Hypotension, or lowering of blood pressure, is associated with dizziness and can be serious for the elderly who may fall and injure themselves. A hypertensive crisis or sudden elevation of blood pressure can occur when MAOI's react with foodstuffs containing tyramine. For this reason, certain foods, drugs, and drinks must be restricted when a patient takes an MAOI (see Chart 14).

When patients, already frightened by the prospect of a panic attack, glance at the *Physicians' Desk Reference*, the list of precautions and adverse reactions of the MAOI's is overwhelming. If patients follow simple rules involving dietary restrictions, their fear is not justified as problems usually do not arise. Dr. Kenneth I. Shulman, at a meeting of the American Psychiatric Association, emphasized that a rational and responsible approach regarding dietary restrictions for MAOI's involves eliminating those foods that are truly dangerous and being more lax with foods for which there is only a case report. As soon as patients learn that a restricted food is actually safe, Dr. Shulman said, "They lose respect for prohibition of the truly dangerous food." Like the TCA's, the MAOI's require two or more weeks before maximal therapeutic dose is reached in the bloodstream. Four to seven weeks must elapse to determine treatment success or failure.

CHART 14

FOODS AND SUBSTANCES TO BE AVOIDED WHEN TAKING MONAMINE OXIDASE INHIBITORS

Foods with significant amounts of tyramine:
> Beer
> Red wines (especially chianti)
> Other alcoholic beverages in large quantities
> Beef or chicken livers
> Brewer's yeast
> Canned figs
> Cheese (non-processed cheese and cream cheese are allowable)
> Fava or broad beans (Italian green beans)
> Game
> Herring
> Summer sausage

The following foods may cause problems when consumed in large quantities:
> Ripe avocado
> Ripe fresh banana
> Sour cream
> Soy sauce
> Yogurt

201

Medications to avoid:
>   Amphetamines ("speed" or "uppers")
>   Anorexiants (appetite suppressants)
>   Certain cold remedies
>   Dopamine hydrochloride
>   Epinephrine, Norepinephrine
>   Nasal decongestants

OTHER ANTIDEPRESSANTS

Although the most widely used and studied anti-depressants are imipramine and phenelzine, there are a number of other TCA's and MAOI's which are effective in controlling panic. These antidepressants differ from one another in chemical composition and side effect profile; however, all are believed to have antipanic properties. When side effects interfere with compliance, it may be worthwhile to switch to another antidepressant.

A newcomer to the antidepressant field is fluoxetine. Although primarily used for depression, recent reports indicate that fluoxetine may be beneficial in panic disorder and obsessive compulsive disorder. Fluoxetine has a different chemical structure when compared to a TCA or an MAOI and the side effects are less severe. If patients cannot tolerate a TCA or an MAOI, it might be desirable to switch to fluoxetine. Fluoxetine is the "new kid on the block" and the research data needs to be bolstered before it is approved by the FDA in the treatment of panic disorder.

Clomipramine has recently been approved for use in obsessive compulsive disorder in the United States.

Since it is a tricyclic antidepressant very similar to imipramine, one would expect that clomipramine would have an antipanic effect. The side effect profile is similar but more severe than that of imipramine. More research has to be completed on clomipramine before it can be recommended for use as an antipanic agent.

BENZODIAZEPINES

Over the past 30 years, benzodiazepines, such as diazepam and chlordiazepoxide have been used to treat anxiety but not panic disorder. In the last ten years, however, a newer benzodiazepine, alprazolam, and more recently clonazepam, have been shown to prevent panic attacks as effectively as imipramine or phenelzine. Generally, patients treated with these two benzodiazepines respond within a few days, and the troublesome side effects found in the TCA's and MAOI's are absent. It has also been demonstrated that anticipatory anxiety, generalized anxiety, and phobias associated with panic disorder respond to treatment with alprazolam and clonazepam. Dr. Robert L. DuPont, clinical professor of psychiatry at Georgetown University School of Medicine, has stated, "Benzodiazepines are among the safest and most effective treatments in all of medicine, including their role in the treatment of panic disorder." Dr. Jonathan R. T. Davidson, director of the Anxiety Disorders Program at Duke University Medical Center has commented that, "The fear of escalating usage of benzodiazepines is unfounded; dosage tends to decrease over time and drug efficacy is maintained."

Alprazolam has many advantages. This antipanic medication acts quickly, has minimal side effects, and good patient compliance. Tolerance usually does not develop and alprazolam is rarely abused by panic disorder patients. Alprazolam is the only antipanic medication approved by the FDA for the treatment of panic disorder. Increased symptoms between dosages have been reported, but "interdose rebound effects" can be minimized when alprazolam is prescribed four times per day. Fearful patients taking alprazolam "clock watch" in an attempt to stave off an attack. These patients are frightened that a panic attack might erupt between dosages. Of course, "clock watching" is worry, an encephalic activity which itself increases anxiety. As is the case with all benzodiazepines, drowsiness is the most common side effect, occurring in four to nine percent of patients. After the first few doses, sedation usually disappears. Ataxia occurs in less than two percent of the patients and other side effects in less than one percent. Abrupt withdrawal of alprazolam can be associated with anxiety, insomnia, irritability, nausea, headaches, palpitations, tremors and, rarely, seizures. When the dosage of alprazolam is slowly reduced, no significant withdrawal symptoms occur.

Clonazepam is another benzodiazepine which has been used successfully to treat panic disorder. Clonazepam is about twice as potent as alprazolam and is a longer acting medication; hence, it needs to be prescribed only twice a day. There is no "interdose rebound effect" (panic-anxiety symptoms between dosages) and patients usually do not "clock watch". Nine percent of patients taking clonazepam report depression as compared to two percent for alprazolam. Preliminary studies indicate equal efficacy for clonazepam when compared to alprazolam. Although it has been reported that other benzodiazepines have been successful in the treatment of panic disorder, further study is required.

At the present time, alprazolam and clonazepam are the two benzodiazepines that are being used extensively for the treatment of panic disorder. Benzodiazepines are among the safest drugs used in medicine and, when taken as prescribed, patients need not fear adverse side effects. Alprazolam and clonazepam may be the mainstay in stopping panic attacks, but as with other antipanic medications, they must be accompanied by psychological interventions to comprehensively treat panic disorder.

CHOICE OF ANTIPANIC MEDICATION

The three groups of medication (TCA's, MAOI's, and benzodiazepines) have proven effective in blocking panic attacks. The choice of drug depends upon the personal proclivities of the physician and the response of the patient. The three types have pros and cons in terms of onset of action, frequency of administration, side effects, and withdrawal problems. It may take several weeks for the TCA's and MAOI's to reach maximal therapeutic level in the bloodstream while the benzodiazepines work almost immediately. To avoid a "rebound effect", alprazolam must be prescribed four times a day. Clonazepam can be dispensed twice a day. The TCA's and MAOI's can be prescribed once or twice a day, and share unpleasant, but usually transitory side effects. With TCA's a "jitteriness syndrome" may occur early in treatment; the MAOI's require certain dietary restrictions. The benzodiazepines have rapid onset of action and very few of the side effects which interfere with patient compliance.

If the antipanic medications are slowly discontinued, usually no problems with withdrawal occur. However, in all three groups a significant relapse rate (resurgence of panic attacks) has been reported when medication is stopped. Pharmacologic treatment is evolving, and undoubtedly new medications will be developed to more effectively treat panic disorder.

My personal preference for treating patients with panic disorder is alprazolam. Alprazolam is safe, easily tolerated by patients, and effective. Most patients receive relief from panic within a few days after taking alprazolam. They also report lower levels of anxiety, fewer physical symptoms, and sometimes less phobic behavior. Because improvement is rapid and occasionally dramatic, patients quickly draw the conclusion that alprazolam will be needed for a lifetime. Alprazolam may enter the fabric of their phobic thinking. Patients' self-statements can include worrisome questions: "What will happen if I do not take the medication on time? What will happen if my doctor discontinues the medication? What will happen if I forget to take the medication?" and,

"What will happen if my prescription runs out?" These anxiety-generating thoughts about alprazolam, as well as other antipanic agents, diminish as treatment progresses and non-pharmacologic methods of coping with anxiety are mastered.

If, for whatever reason, a panic patient refuses or cannot tolerate alprazolam, my next choice is imipramine. To minimize side effects, I start patients on a low dose. Patients are told about the two or three week delay in reaching a therapeutic level of this TCA in the bloodstream. If panic attacks continue, the dosage is raised in small increments until an antipanic level is reached. Imipramine also has antidepressant properties which are very helpful for panic patients with depression.

If alprazolam and imipramine fail to block panic attacks, a third alternative is phenelzine, a MAOI. I hesitate to prescribe MAOI's because of the fear some panic patients develop when side effects are explained and a list of forbidden foodstuffs provided. Just mentioning the possibility of a "hypertensive crisis" is enough to scare off even a brave panic-prone patient. Other physicians may not share my concern regarding the MAOI's and certainly, if precautions are taken, this class of medication can be very effective in stopping panic attacks.

DURATION OF MEDICATION TREATMENT

How long should a patient be maintained on an antipanic medication? This question cannot be answered with certainty; it depends upon multiple factors. In panic and agoraphobia, the three classes of symptoms are: (1) panic attacks, (2) the phobic reaction of avoidance, and (3) phobic thinking. The decision to discontinue medication is intimately tied to the reduction of symptoms from all three sources. Medication stops panic attacks. Exposure treats the phobic reaction of avoidance. Encephalic intervention helps to change phobic thinking, and other psychological interventions reduce the general level of stress and anxiety. When these goals have been achieved and patients have experienced no panic attacks in the previous six months, slow withdrawal from antipanic medication can begin. Dr. Russell Noyes, Jr., professor of psychiatry at the University of Iowa, has stated that medication should be sustained for six to twelve months and then gradually tapered. Repeated relapses may indicate the need for indefinite continuation.

Phobic thinking is perhaps the biggest obstacle to successful withdrawal from antipanic medication. The mere mention of a decrease in dose often causes an immediate increase in anxiety. "What if the panic attacks come back? What if I get worse?" These self-statements increase anxiety BEFORE the dosage of medication has even been reduced. At times, doctors wrongfully attribute these psychological cognitive symptoms to the effects of physiological withdrawal from medication. For this reason, it is best to slowly reduce the dosage of the antipanic agent so patients can accommodate their thinking to adjustments in medication.

Patients sometimes misinterpret the anxiety associated with the slow reduction of medication as a signal that a panic attack might erupt immediately. To counter the apprehension about a relapse, a plan must be developed to deal with any anxiety related to withdrawal. Patients can be instructed to cope with withdrawal anxiety by utilizing progressive muscle relaxation and encephalic interventions (thought stopping, thought substitution, and the four positive reinforcing statements). Once experience has demonstrated that nothing serious or irreversible will happen as the dose of medication is reduced, fearful thoughts and anxiety diminish.

If panic attacks recur as the dose of antipanic agent is lowered, patients must be reassured that medication will be reinstated. Sometimes frightened patients misinterpret anxiety as panic and only need reassurance. Also, one panic attack is not a sufficient reason to stop the withdrawal program. It is only when panic attacks erupt frequently and are accompanied by a resurgence of phobic behavior that antipanic medication must again be prescribed. Physicians and patients should answer the following question: Is it better to take no medication and experience repeated panic attacks and other severe symptoms, or to take medication and be symptom-free? The answer in my mind is obvious. The alleviation of suffering has always been a physician's primary role. For some patients, long term use of medication may be required. As far as we know, there are no permanent side effects of the TCA's, MAOI's, or benzodiazepines when these medications are taken in prescribed dosages by healthy people. Of course, prudence requires that patients be monitored on a regular basis by their physician. There is no question that medication offers the quickest and surest method to conquer panic attacks. The ideal goal is for a person to be medication-free. When withdrawal is combined with psychological intervention, many patients can reach this ultimate goal.

RELAXATION TREATMENT

One of the most striking and frightening features of a panic attack is the feeling of helplessness reported by most victims. The sudden eruption of intense, uncontrollable symptoms seemingly from out of the blue affects both mind and body. After the attack, victims are shaken and confused. The state of uncertainty (not knowing if and when another attack will strike) leads sufferers to worry, thus increasing anxiety and the vulnerability to another panic attack.

Instead of being a passive victim waiting defenselessly for a panic attack to erupt, relaxation techniques afford patients a method of gaining control over panic symptoms. Progressive muscle relaxation (PMR) and related techniques such as meditation, self-hypnosis, autogenic training, and even prayer, impact on the mind and body. These methods enhance relaxation in the muscles, facilitate soothing respiratory sensations, produce warm feelings in the abdomen, calm troublesome thoughts, and are associated with a pervasive feeling of well-being. PMR, as well as the time-tested methods mentioned, produce an inner feeling of composure and self-control which are incompatible with anxiety. As one learns the technique of PMR, control and eventual mastery over anxiety replaces a feeling of powerlessness.

THE TECHNIQUE OF MUSCLE RELAXATION

Many systems of muscle relaxation exist, but most are variations of Dr. Edmund Jacobson's method. The following instructions to a patient are my adaptation of Jacobson's procedure. The instructions are shorter, but in my experience, just as effective as the longer version.

1. Select a quiet, dimly illuminated room and sit in a favorite chair or lie on a soft bed. Loosen your clothing so that you are completely comfortable. Stretch, then let your body go limp. Eliminate any distractions from your environment.

2. Make a tight fist with your right hand and concentrate on the tense feelings in that hand, wrist, and forearm. After five seconds, open your fist and concentrate on the relaxing, tingly or heavy sensations in your right hand, wrist, and forearm. Repeat this several times and then move on to the left hand and redo the sequence.

3. Next, shrug your shoulders upwards towards your ears and at the same time towards the center of your body. Hold that tense position for five seconds. Release the tension, pause, notice the feelings of relaxation in your shoulders and upper arms. Repeat the same procedure several times. (Be careful not to do these

exercises too vigorously. You may get a muscle cramp. Although this is not serious, it may be temporarily distracting.)

4. Now, take a deep breath, hold it, count to five, and slowly exhale. Repeat this maneuver several times. Deep breathing is an important part of relaxation. As you breathe out, note that your entire body seemingly sinks into the surface that you are lying upon and the feeling of relaxation becomes more pronounced and wide-spread.

5. Contract your stomach muscles by pushing them outward. Count to five then relax the abdominal muscles. Notice a warm, glowing, and tingling sensation in the stomach area. Repeat this procedure several times.

6. Now, move on to your lower extremities, the legs. Bend your ankles so that your feet move toward the floor. Hold that position for five seconds then release the tension. Next, bend your ankles so that your feet move toward your head. Hold that position for the count of five then release the pressure. Repeat both exercises several times.

7. Press both shoulders backwards and arch your back about one inch off the surface you are lying on. Hold that position for five seconds and then release the tension. In this way, the upper and lower back can be tensed and then relaxed. Be careful if you have a history of back problems.

8. Next, the neck muscles can be tensed, then relaxed. Press your head backwards until you meet resistance. Maintain that position for the count of five then release the tension. Next, bend your head forward with your chin towards your chest. Hold it for five seconds then release the pressure. Now, move your head so that your left ear moves toward your left shoulder. Hold that position for five seconds then let your head move into a neutral position. Do the same for the right side. Repeat the four exercises until your neck muscles are completely relaxed.

9. The facial muscles are usually under a great deal of tension. Take your time and repeat the various exercises as often as necessary to relax your facial muscles. First, raise your eyebrows upwards, wrinkling your forehead. Hold it for five seconds and then release the tension. Next, move your eyebrows down as if in a frown. Hold it for five seconds then release the pressure. Repeat this procedure several times until your forehead is completely relaxed.

10. If you wear contact lenses, remove them before attempting the following eye exercises. With your eyes remaining closed, first look straight ahead, then to your extreme left, hold it for five seconds, and then look straight ahead. Repeat the same procedure, this time to the right. Next, beginning with your eyes in a neutral position, look up, hold it for five

seconds then look straight ahead. Now, look down hold it for five seconds then look straight ahead. Finally, close your eyes very tightly, hold it for five seconds then release the pressure until your eyes remain comfortably closed.

11. The masseter or jaw muscle is the strongest muscle of the face and is often under considerable tension. First, bite down hard on your back teeth (the molars) and maintain the bite while counting to five then release the pressure. Repeat the jaw exercise several times, concluding with your mouth and teeth slightly separated.

12. If any muscles still seem tense, go back to that muscle group and repeat the exercise until those muscles are completely relaxed.

The skill of progressive muscle relaxation is easy to acquire, but it does require practice. Relaxation treatment reduces the tendency to anticipate anxiety and to misinterpret body sensations as symptoms of disease. Panic-agoraphobic patients feel out of control and at the mercy of panic and anxiety. Relaxation treatment affords a means of reducing panic and anxiety thus restoring the important element of control. Pre-recorded instructional audio-cassettes facilitate the learning of relaxation and are available at most bookstores.

PASSIVE RELAXATION TECHNIQUE

Passive relaxation (PR), a variant of self-hypnosis, can be practiced without tensing and contracting the muscle groups of the body. First, the subject takes three, slow, deep breaths to begin the process. Next, attention is paid to the toes and feet, and the patient concentrates on any warm, tingly feelings which are present. These feelings are identified as relaxation sensations and through concentration, the sensations move from the feet to the legs, hips, stomach, chest, back, shoulders, arms, hands, fingers, neck, and head. Afterwards, relaxation is intensified by visualizing — clearly and vividly — pleasant scenes such as lying on the beach, walking through a flower-laden garden, or perhaps a prearranged scene which elicits peaceful and restful feelings. A counting sequence of ten to zero with interspersed suggestions of relaxation may be used to deepen the relaxed state. Although PR can best be done with the eyes closed and in a recumbent position, it can be practiced with the eyes open and in any position (sitting or standing). The advantage of PR over PMR is that it is not obvious to others, so it can be utilized to reduce anxiety in public situations. PR requires concentration and, once learned, is a valuable tool in controlling mental processes leading to the lowering of anxiety.

The technique of relaxation, once acquired, can be used over a lifetime and has prophylactic value in warding off stress and anxiety. Relaxation reduces panic and diminishes the physiologic symptoms of anxiety. When symptoms of panic or anxiety occur, it becomes a signal to employ techniques of muscle relaxation. Rather than being at the mercy of their symptoms, panic-prone patients can exert conscious control over symptoms as relaxation replaces help-lessness.

CONCLUSIONS

In panic disorder, medication and relaxation may be all that are needed for successful treatment. This is especially true when panic and agoraphobia are not of long duration. If phobic thinking has not become ingrained and agoraphobic symptoms are minimal, patients may respond quickly to medication and relaxation. Other treatment methods may not be required.

Part VI

Overcoming Agoraphobia

The Greek is No Longer Phobic

16

Treatment of Agoraphobia

No longer fearful of the agora, the Greek mingles freely with other people as he bargains for goods. Relaxed and confident in the marketplace, the Greek has overcome agoraphobia. Anyone with agoraphobia can follow the Greek's example.

The rewards for overcoming agoraphobia are many. Independence is restored. Marital and family relationships improve. Work is more gratifying. Managing a household becomes easier. As the restrictions imposed by agoraphobia diminish, phobic boundaries dissolve. Travel and vacations turn into a source of pleasure. Victims formerly perceived as unfriendly, withdrawn, or strange can now interact normally with others as cure leads to improved social and recreational activities. Virtually all areas of life which have been affected by agoraphobia can be improved by treatment.

The concept of the Three E's is a format upon which therapeutic interventions are based. This chapter amplifies treatment strategies and techniques that have been mentioned earlier. Success in overcoming agoraphobia depends upon a systematic application of these psychological interventions.

A prerequisite for overcoming agoraphobia is control and eventual cessation of panic and limited symptom attacks. Panic attacks perpetuate fear and promote phobic avoidance. As was mentioned in Chapter 15, antipanic medication prescribed in therapeutic doses will block panic attacks and control anxiety symptoms. When panic or limited symptom attacks no longer occur, it is far easier to implement other components of therapy.

Learning relaxation is also essential. Agoraphobics are exquisitely sensitive to symptoms which remind them of panic. Relaxation treatment affords an immediate means of reducing anxiety related symptoms and restoring the important element of confidence. It is comforting for agoraphobics to have at their disposal a self-generating technique which lowers anxiety and deters panic and limited symptom attacks. Relaxation, once learned, can be employed anywhere and any time. A complete description of the technique is to be found in the previous chapter.

ENVIRONMENTAL INTERVENTIONS

SELF-EDUCATION

Misunderstandings and myths about agoraphobia abound. Irrational symptoms confuse patients, causing them to feel embarrassed or even ashamed. Knowledge is power, and the power of comprehending agoraphobia helps sufferers overcome it. Misconceptions about agoraphobia must be dispelled as a prologue to treatment. I have always believed that part of my responsibility as a physician is to educate my patients by explaining the etiology and proposed treatment of their disorder. I invite the spouse or significant other to attend sessions devoted to education and explanation about agoraphobia. I also encourage my patients to read books and attend meetings concerning panic and agoraphobia.

COMMONLY ASKED QUESTIONS ABOUT AGORAPHOBIA

1. Are my parents responsible for my disorder?

Answer: It is important to understand that although parents may have contributed to the development of agoraphobia, they should not be blamed for it. Time is wasted on the exercise of culpability, and it is more beneficial to forget the past and concentrate on current pathologic behavior.

2. My doctors tell me that there is nothing wrong with me physically. Why do I keep experiencing physical symptoms?

Answer: Panic and limited symptom attacks are neuro-physiologically produced and do not indicate a physical disease. Many patients misinterpret discharge of the nervous system as evidence of physical illness. Rapid heart beat, shortness of breath, dizziness, and other symptoms are due to anxiety. The results of a physical examination and laboratory tests will clearly indicate if something is physically wrong.

3. Why do I have difficulty leaving my home?

Answer: One of the main characteristics of agoraphobia is the inability to move freely within the community. As the agoraphobic patient leaves his/her home, anxiety mounts roughly in proportion to distance or time from the home. At some point, anxiety becomes so intense that the patient feels compelled to return home quickly. This retreat is associated with a decrease in anxiety which acts to reinforce avoidance behavior. Home becomes associated with a safe haven and leaving home is fraught with fear.

4. Why do I feel nervous when I am in a church, a movie theatre, or a restaurant?

Answer: Most agoraphobics experience intense anxiety when they are in situations where they feel "trapped". Attendance at public gatherings, especially if seated up front and away from exits, stimulates thoughts of being a public spectacle if a panic attack strikes. Agoraphobics fear that they will faint, lose control, or go crazy. This never happens; nevertheless, agoraphobics are plagued by this possibility and avoid situations where escape to a safe haven is hampered.

5. Why do I feel the need to always be accompanied by my spouse when I leave home?

Answer: When patients are accompanied by a spouse, it changes the way they think. Frantic, anxiety-evoking thoughts are replaced by the reassuring thought that if something bad should happen, the spouse can take charge. Insistence about being accompanied is a form of phobic avoidance and must be dealt with during treatment. It should not be forgotten that irrational requests foster dependency.

6. Will this treatment program get to the root of my problem?

Answer: There is a genesis of agoraphobia to be sure, but the concept that effective therapy depends on uncovering the root or core of agoraphobia is fallacious, as is the belief that symptom substitution will occur if this is not done. By employing the treatment methods discussed in this chapter, symptoms are alleviated and patients begin feeling better in other areas of their lives.

7. Am I crazy?

Answer: Agoraphobic patients are in contact with reality and know that their behavior is irrational. Because they are embarrassed by their behavior, agoraphobics try to conceal their disorder from others. They frequently rationalize and practice self-deception. Depression is common in agoraphobia. Their lives become more and more constricted and they occasionally turn to alcohol or other sedative drugs for relief. Family relationships and work performance suffer as anxiety and phobic behavior take over. At the beginning of treatment, agoraphobics have a lot of problems; however, they are not crazy and do not suffer from psychosis.

8. Why do I fear traveling?

Answer: This is part of the agoraphobic's reluctance to leave the security of home. Since vehicles are used to leave home, phobias of traveling in cars, buses, trains, or airplanes often are part of the clinical picture. Agoraphobics fear that they may be struck down at any time by a panic or limited symptom attack, leaving them helpless in a strange place. This uncertainty results in a reluctance or refusal to travel.

9. A doctor tells me that I am in good physical health. How can he be so sure?

Answer: After performing a physical examination and completing all necessary laboratory tests, a physician can give you an appraisal of your physical health. In addition, when the diagnosis of agoraphobia is made, the doctor knows that an irrational concern for physical health is part of that syndrome. In the final analysis, the ultimate proof lies in the fact that physical symptoms abate or disappear as treatment progresses.

10. Once I am cured, will my symptoms ever come back?

Answer: In agoraphobia, as in all other medical and mental disorders, there is a possibility that symptoms might recur. That is the bad news. The good news is that if patients adhere to a relapse prevention program, recurrence can be minimized. It should not be forgotten that what worked before will work again. A reinstatement of the treatment program usually produces good results. It has been my experience that if a patient relapses, subsequent treatment is effective and of shorter duration.

ENHANCED COMMUNICATION

All illness impacts upon the family of the patient. Lack of communication with friends and relatives adds to stress and anxiety. Sharing information about agoraphobia with the family enhances communication and facilitates treatment. Each of the questions mentioned in the previous section must be discussed in order to correct any misconceptions. Enhanced communication closes the information gap, restores family harmony, and removes obstacles to treatment.

EXPOSURE TREATMENT

Exposure is extremely effective in the treatment of agoraphobia. For those who have confidence and courage, unaccompanied *in vivo* exposure can be self-directed. During the early stages of treatment, therapist-assisted exposure is an acceptable alternative for patients who are too fearful to begin alone. Another option is group exposure treatment. Agoraphobia self-help organizations conduct group exposure, which for some patients can prove to be the bridge to solo exposure. If all of the preceding methods fail, imaginal exposure, as discussed later in this chapter, may be necessary before severe agoraphobics will attempt exposure in real life. Patients must eventually proceed alone through all phases of the exposure treatment program.

The first step of exposure treatment is the development of a hierarchy of situations involving distance or time spent away from a secure area, usually the home (see Table 15). Beginning with the least anxiety-evoking situation, agoraphobics must walk or drive the stated distance away from home, repeating that step as often as necessary until anxiety diminishes. As a general rule, the longer the agoraphobic remains in the phobic situation, the more effective is exposure treatment. At the conclusion of each step, the patient must feel reasonably calm before proceeding to the next item in the hierarchy.

CHART 15

TYPICAL HIERARCHY FOR AGORAPHOBIA FROM LOW TO HIGH ANXIETY

		Time Away From Home, Minutes
1.	You are at home thinking about leaving unaccompanied.	
2.	You leave your home and walk to the street.	
3.	You walk 1 block from home.	1
4.	You walk 3 blocks from home.	3
5.	You walk 5 blocks from home.	5
6.	You walk 10 blocks from home.	10
7.	You walk 18 blocks from home.	12
8.	You walk 25 blocks from home.	20
9.	You walk 30 blocks from home.	28
10.	You walk 35 blocks from home.	35
11.	You walk 40 blocks from home.	50
12.	You walk 45 blocks from home.	60

Desensitization will not take place if the patient leaves home and goes the required distance, but returns lickety-split in panic. When this happens, distressing thoughts race through the mind. "I was lucky that I didn't have a panic attack. I made it today, but I'm not sure about the next time. If I went farther, I'm certain I would have fainted." Returning home in an anxious state erases any gains. The length of time and the number of times that a patient spends in the phobic situation is correlated with success. A therapeutic session of exposure treatment should always end with the patient in a state of relative calm and with a feeling of accomplishment.

Exposure treatment causes some anxiety, but it is temporary and always less than an agoraphobic anticipates. During the exposure session, existing anxiety can be controlled with relaxation techniques, thought stopping, thought substitution, as well as the four positive reinforcing statements. If panic or a limited symptom attack occurs during exposure treatment, it does not mean that this form of treatment must be discontinued. Rather, by adjusting the dosage of antipanic medication upward and the distance gradient of the hierarchy downward, exposure treatment continues without interruption. Minor setbacks should be expected. Progress, if plotted on a piece of graph paper, would not be a straight upward line. More likely, improvement would include small dips downward from time to time. When progress is averaged, however, an upward curve would dominate the graph.

Footdragging is the chief obstacle to success during exposure treatment. Fear, sometimes camouflaged by rationalization, promotes procrastination. Habits are hard to break, and the well established habit of phobic avoidance does not yield easily. This is especially true at the beginning of exposure treatment. Agoraphobics tend to dwell on the possibility of a panic attack, thereby increasing anxiety and the proclivity to procrastinate. Engaging in exposure treatment once or twice a day and remaining in the phobic situation for increasingly longer periods of time, breaks the avoidance pattern by the process of desensitization.

Keeping a daily diary during exposure treatment helps to minimize procrastination and places progress in perspective. As the agoraphobic reviews each week, improvement generally overshadows any minor mishap. Frightened patients often concentrate on the difficult days, ignoring the trend of improvement. It is one of the paradoxes of life that people focus on negative life experiences while ignoring or minimizing positive gains. This human tendency distorts therapeutic outcome and erodes the confidence of patients.

Some agoraphobics resist exposure treatment because they structure their lives within the boundaries of their phobia. Shopping trips, vacations, and excursions to visit friends or relatives are delayed or avoided. Rationalization prevails. Shopping is not necessary. A vacation would not be fun and is too expensive. Sooner or later friends and relatives will visit. Unless the agoraphobic feels strongly dissatisfied with their lifestyle, the desire to change may be weak. Outcome of exposure treatment is determined by several factors: (1) motivation to change, (2) frequency of exposure, and (3) time spent in the phobic situation. Those agoraphobics who approach exposure treatment with true grit and steadfastness can expect a good outcome.

A patient of mine developed panic disorder with agoraphobia when she was a 16-year-old high school student. Because of repeated panic attacks which evolved into agoraphobia, she quit high school and, for 10 years, rarely left home. On occasion, she would visit relatives if her parents accompanied her. This limited life style was supported by her father and mother who liked having her around the house. After reading some articles about agoraphobia in the newspaper, she called for an appointment and appeared in my office with her parents. She no longer had panic attacks but was severely agoraphobic. Strongly motivated to change, the young woman diligently followed the plan of exposure treatment. Each day she ventured farther and farther from home, utilizing techniques of relaxation, thought stopping, and thought substitution to reduce anxiety. She kept a diary of her experiences during exposure treatment which was reviewed at each treatment session. Problems which occasionally arose were resolved and exposure treatment proceeded two to three times a day. After several months passed, she was traveling freely around the city. Eventually, she finished high school and entered college. Working part time while attending school, she accumulated enough money to get an apartment. She began traveling, first by car and then by airplane, to visit friends and go on vacations. She has overcome agoraphobia, and today is a self-confident and independent woman.

When formal exposure treatment has been completed, less structured exposure can be undertaken. Visiting friends, walking in a park, shopping, or other activities which formerly evoked anxiety, become the target for future exposure. The pleasure derived from these excursions accelerates the curative process.

Agoraphobics frequently have specific phobias such as using elevators, driving an automobile, riding in boats, or flying in airplanes. These phobias often diminish or disappear as patients are successfully desensitized using the main hierarchy of distance from home. If the particular fear persists, exposure treatment continues, utilizing a new hierarchy developed for the specific phobia. For example, Chart 16 is a typical hierarchy for the fear of flying. Exposure treatment is accomplished fairly quickly for specific phobias, especially if the patient is strongly motivated to change for reasons of business or pleasure.

CHART 16

FEAR OF FLYING HIERARCHY
FROM LOW TO HIGH ANXIETY

1. You are at home thinking about the prospects of a trip by airplane.
2. You have decided to take an airplane flight and have made arrangements by ordering tickets and planning your trip.
3. It is now the day of your airplane flight and you are at home packing and preparing.
4. You have loaded your luggage in your automobile and are driving to the airport.
5. You arrive at the airport and are entering the terminal, walking to the airline counter, finalizing your ticket, and checking your baggage.
6. You are walking to the departure gate, passing the security check, and going to the airline counter to receive your boarding pass.
7. You are waiting to board your flight.
8. Your flight has been called and you enter the aircraft, select a seat, and fasten your seat belt.
9. The aircraft door has been closed, the engines have been started, and the aircraft begins to taxi to the head of the runway.
10. The aircraft takes off (describe all physical sensations).
11. The airplane is climbing to cruising altitude which is reached in a short time, and the "fasten seat belt" and "no smoking" signs go off.
12. Your aircraft is flying in calm weather, but now enters some turbulence for several minutes, and then your flight again becomes calm.
13. Your aircraft lands without incident.
14. You depart the airplane, looking forward to your next trip.

ENCEPHALIC INTERVENTIONS

PHOBIC THINKING

All victims of panic and agoraphobia, to some extent, possess the self-defeating habit of phobic or catastrophic thinking. They imagine dreadful consequences to ordinary life events. Like smoking, overeating, or biting one's fingernails, phobic thinking has a compulsive quality and is difficult to control. Unlike most habits, phobic thinking is a mental practice which cannot be directly observed. Contrary to the cigarette smoker who mentally wrestles with the impulse to light-up, or the obese person who struggles with the desire to eat, the agoraphobic, lacking insight, easily falls prey to the habit of phobic thinking.

The old, anxiety-evoking videotapes of the mind have been programmed by panic. For example, going to church ordinarily elicits thoughts and visual images of quiet contemplation. For an agoraphobic, a suggestion to attend a religious service brings forth mental images of losing control and becoming a spectacle in front of the congregation. Prayerful communion leading to peace of mind is supplanted by phobic thinking. Similarly, going on vacation, visiting friends, and attending movies are viewed by agoraphobics as threatening. Phobic thinking is an almost automatic response to any situation which falls outside of a defined "safety zone", or has the potential of producing a "trapped feeling". Rather than presage pleasure, agoraphobics conjure up a bad outcome to activities which should be relaxing and enjoyable.

233

Ridding one's self of the habit of phobic thinking is difficult, but it can be done. Smokers quit cigarettes. Obese people lose weight. And once aware of the vicious nature of phobic thinking, agoraphobics can change their cognitions. Thought stopping, thought substitution, and use of the four positive reinforcing statements are encephalic interventions which can break the pernicious habit of phobic thinking.

Thought Stopping and Thought Substitution

Before one can utilize thought stopping techniques, the old anxiety-generating videotapes of the mind must be identified. Recognition of anxious thoughts, followed by the rapid employment of the silently shouted statement, "Stop, get out of there!" is a prerequisite for success. Sometimes agoraphobics feel discouraged when they employ thought stopping because the old thoughts still pop up from time to time. Initially, the goal is to reduce the time spent thinking about negative and anxiety-evoking things by 20 to 30 percent. Significant benefits of thought stopping are noticeable almost immediately and accrue with time.

Thought substitution is a companion to thought stopping. After anxious ideas are driven from the mind, new, pleasing, and relaxing thoughts are substituted. For example, in contemplating a vacation, the positive mental scenarios should emphasize the excitement of seeing new places and meeting new people. Phobic patients should mentally rehearse situations which were formerly associated with anxiety by highlighting anticipated pleasure. Coping with phobic thoughts by accentuating that everything will turn out all right, forms the basis of encephalic reconditioning.

THE FOUR POSITIVE REINFORCING STATEMENTS

During the early stages of treatment, panic-agoraphobic symptoms will appear from time to time. Rather than succumb to symptoms and presage panic, a wiser practice is to interpret anxiety as a signal to employ the four positive reinforcing statements. Statement one, "I feel uncomfortable," acknowledges the fact that physiologic symptoms are not imaginary but reflect anxiety. The second and third statements, "I've had these symptoms before and THEY ALWAYS PASS," and, "There is nothing physically wrong with me," lead to the correct interpretation of symptoms. The fourth statement, "I am experiencing pathologic anxiety," sets the stage for the employment of relaxation techniques. Deep breathing, combined with relaxation of the various muscles, will decrease the intensity of anxiety. This does not happen instantaneously, but relief from anxiety should be expected within one or two minutes (10 or more slow deep breaths).

Another technique involves distraction. Engaging in an activity which involves directing positive mental attention away from physical symptoms decreases anxiety. Talking to another person about enjoyable things or engaging in an activity which requires concentration, can derail negative thoughts. With practice, utilization of the four positive reinforcing statements, coupled with distraction, becomes an almost automatic response to panic and anxiety symptoms.

IMAGINAL EXPOSURE

Most panic and agoraphobic patients spend an excessive amount of time visualizing themselves succumbing to some imagined threat. Agoraphobics are sensitized or made worse by this anxiety-generating visual process which sustains irrational fear. This maladaptive habit perpetuates phobias and other anxious behavior. Imaginal exposure, also called systematic desensitization, utilizes imagination to rid one's self of phobic and inappropriate anxiety. It is a stepping stone for those phobics who cannot engage in real life exposure. As with *in vivo* exposure, a hierarchy is constructed prior to imaginal exposure. The procedure for imaginal exposure is as follows:

Select a room where you will not be disturbed. Sit or lie on a comfortable piece of furniture and get completely relaxed. Begin by visualizing for about 20 seconds the least anxiety-evoking item on the hierarchy. "I am at home thinking about leaving my house unaccompanied." At the end of 20 seconds, take a deep breath, hold it, count to five, then slowly exhale and relax. Counting to five helps to dispel the imagined scene from the mind and allows one to concentrate on relaxation. The scene is repeated until it can be visualized without anxiety. At this point, the next scene is introduced and the same procedure is repeated.

Treatment continues systematically until all anxiety-evoking scenes in the hierarchy can be visualized without significant anxiety (see Table 15).

At the beginning of imaginal exposure, some agoraphobics have a tendency to anticipate and visualize the most anxiety-evoking scene. This will result in very high anxiety and defeats the gradual step-by-step process of desensitization. The tendency to anticipate can be conquered with practice. Generally, one should not proceed to more anxiety-evoking items on the hierarchy until the previous scene is mastered.

Another mistake is incorrect visualization. Rather than picturing the fearful scene, some phobics say to themselves, "I know I am at home as I am visualizing this scene and nothing bad can happen to me." In fact, agoraphobics are experts in visualizing inappropriate, anxiety-evoking scenes while in the safety of their home. On many occasions, they have visualized going shopping or visiting friends and become so fearful and anxious that they refuse to leave home. The realistic visualization of phobic scenes during imaginal exposure treatment counter-conditions anxiety and prepares patients for the real thing. Improper visualization can be easily corrected with practice and usually poses no problem once the technique has been explained and rehearsed.

A further difficulty which might be encountered during imaginal exposure is the inclusion of groundless fears. Losing control, going crazy, or having a heart attack may be unintentionally included in the imagined scene. Each item on the hierarchy must be visualized so that the scene represents a successful confrontation with the phobic situation. It must be remembered that nothing really tragic happens when agoraphobics travel increasing distances from home or remain in so-called "trapped situations" for long periods of time.

The coping strategies employed during imaginal exposure are the same that will be used in real life. These include: deep breathing to combat undue anxiety, thought stopping and substitution to control unwanted mental activity, and the use of the four positive reinforcing statements to correct misconceptions about physical sensations. Most importantly, at the conclusion of each imaginal exposure session, the agoraphobic must feel a subjective sense of improvement. When anxiety goes down during desensitization, the resulting sense of calmness leads to a feeling of confidence. Agoraphobics must, of course, test themselves by *in vivo* exposure, utilizing the same hierarchy developed during imaginal exposure.

Imaginal exposure is mental rehearsal for the real thing. Prior to giving a lecture, I mentally rehearse my presentation. I picture the time, the place, and the audience. I also visualize that I am delivering a good speech which is received with enthusiasm. Imaginal exposure, like mental rehearsal, can be part of preparation for any new performance or activity which is associated with anxiety. As in most skills that we learn in life, practice, if not making it perfect, does make it easier.

A CASE HISTORY

The following account is not extraordinary. I see patients like this every day. This case history represents many agoraphobics across the country who come under treatment and recover.

Ann, a mother of three children, had been married to a lawyer for ten years. Her chief complaint was a fear of leaving home by herself. If left alone at home, she thought she might die of a heart attack. Ann also feared using elevators, escalators, airplanes, and avoided small rooms, crowds, bridges, expressways, and would not drive a car.

Three years prior to her consultation, Ann was hospitalized for severe pneumonia. While recovering in the hospital, she developed chest pain, a rapidly beating heart, difficulties in breathing, and high anxiety. When she complained to a nurse, a cardiologist was immediately summoned. After a physical examination and an electrocardiogram, she was told that she had mitral valve prolapse, but otherwise her heart was normal. She was puzzled about the diagnosis. No explanation or treatment was offered despite the fact that she continued to have intermittent chest pain, palpitations, shortness of breath, dizziness, and bursts of anxiety.

Following her discharge from the hospital, some of Ann's symptoms continued. She consulted several doctors, all of whom concluded that there was no evidence of cardiac disease. She was told that mitral valve prolapse was a relatively innocuous condition that did not require treatment. After each examination, Ann was momentarily reassured; however, her symptoms continued and doubts about the adequacy of her doctors grew. Panic attacks periodically erupted while she was shopping or driving. At times, she would have to quit shopping, abandon her automobile, and make a frantic phone call to her husband, pleading for him to rescue her. As panic attacks occurred more frequently, she refused to leave home unless accompanied by her husband or a trusted friend. Eventually, she became so panicky that she could not stay home alone; consequently, a live-in maid was hired. She became housebound.

Ann's past history disclosed that as a child she was shy, self-conscious, and anxious. During puberty, these characteristics intensified and crystallized into an "inferiority complex". At age 14, Ann saw a psychiatrist for one year because of nervousness. She benefited from this experience and felt more confident and less anxious. While in college, she met her future husband and after one year of courtship they were married. Over the course of the next ten years, Ann gave birth to three healthy children and was relatively happy.

The patient's family history disclosed that Ann's father, the president of a large corporation, was a quiet and stern man who, she related, punished her by withdrawing love and verbal expressions of approval. Even today, the patient said, her father, though quite old, has a foreboding demeanor and she is still somewhat frightened of him. Ann described her mother as a fear-ridden woman who has had heart disease most of her life. She felt that her mother and father had never loved one another. Although her parents had never been physically abusive, Ann sensed disapproval and loss of love, feelings which were particularly strong during her formative years.

Ann's problems were analyzed as follows. She appeared to have a hereditary predisposition for anxiety which made her vulnerable to panic attacks. Prior to entering the hospital for pneumonia, she was under a considerable amount of stress related to marital conflicts and problems with her children. The additional stress and anxiety associated with her acute illness pushed her over the brink, and in the hospital she had a panic attack. Doctors, more concerned with Ann's physical health, failed to diagnose and treat the panic symptoms. Upon discharge from the hospital, she continued to have panic-anxiety symptoms, leaving her puzzled and alarmed. Frequent consultations with doctors, who concluded that she was physically sound, led to only momentary reassurance. "How can this be true?", thought Ann, as she was continuing to suffer from panic symptoms. As panic attacks erupted more frequently, Ann became phobic and began to avoid an increasing number of situations and activities. She could not function adequately as a wife or a mother, and steered clear of most social and recreational activities. Ann became housebound and felt miserable.

TREATMENT

1. *Education and Enhanced Communication* — Ann was told that her condition was due to anxiety and she was suffering from panic disorder with agoraphobia. Results of her medical examinations and laboratory tests were reviewed. It was emphasized that she was physically sound, and her symptoms were anxiety-based. An explanation of the Three E's clarified the source of her panic-anxiety symptoms. Although her vulnerability to panic attacks was probably hereditary, Ann was told that her condition was definitely treatable. The rationale of various elements of treatment was fully discussed.

   During several sessions focusing on enhanced communication, Ann's husband participated in discussions involving panic and agoraphobia, existing marital conflicts, and their children's problems. Ann's unhealthy dependency relationship with her husband became the focus during this phase of therapy. An explanation about the nature of panic and agoraphobia was related to concepts underlying treatment. The husband was told that he inadvertently reinforced his wife's phobia by complying with her irrational requests to return home when she experienced panic-anxiety symptoms. The husband was asked to discontinue this practice and encourage his wife to use PMR, encephalic reconditioning, and exposure treatment. In this way, Ann would become desensitized and more self-reliant. The husband was very cooperative and enthusiastically participated in treatment. Understanding the need for exposure treatment, he accompanied Ann to movies, church, and social engagements. As she began to improve, the husband was overjoyed and praised her lavishly. Toward the end of treatment, he took Ann on a long overdue vacation. The husband's active involvement in treatment unquestionably hastened Ann's recovery.

2. *Medication* — At the beginning of treatment, Ann was placed on an antipanic agent. She remained on medication until she successfully completed exposure treatment. The dosage was gradually decreased over a period of two months, then discontinued.

3. *Relaxation Treatment* — Ann quickly learned the technique of progressive muscle relaxation. If she felt her heart beating fast or noticed any manifestation of anxiety, she employed relaxation to diminish these symptoms. Control replaced fear, and her confidence grew. As treatment progressed, she utilized relaxation whenever she felt tense or nervous in any situation.

4. *Encephalic Reconditioning* — After she was discharged from the hospital, Ann was in good physical health. However, when Ann experienced anxiety symptoms, she thought that she was having a heart attack and would die. Her symptoms in reality, were due to panic and agoraphobia. Reciting the four positive reinforcing statements placed Ann's symptoms in perspective and directed her to utilize relaxation treatment. If anxiety-evoking thoughts intruded on her mind during the day, she was encouraged to employ thought stopping and thought substitution. The old videotapes of the mind picturing fear, panic, anxiety, and futility, were replaced. The new mental videotapes featured her successfully coping with these unpleasant symptoms. Ann also visualized feeling confident that she could handle future situations.

5. *Imaginal Exposure Treatment* — Because Ann was fearful of exposing herself to real life phobic situations, imaginal exposure was started utilizing a hierarchy similar to that shown in Table 15. Successful completion of imaginal exposure treatment required several months. She had difficulty imagining that she could cope with phobic situations since panic-anxiety symptoms entered her mind at unexpected times. However, Ann persisted with imaginal exposure and proceeded to *in vivo* (real life) exposure.

6. *Exposure Treatment* — Prior to her illness, Ann was an exercise enthusiast so she chose walking rather than driving during exposure treatment. Beginning with the lowest anxiety-evoking situation in the hierarchy, she gradually increased her distance from home. While walking alone, she complied with instructions to remain in each situation of the hierarchy until her anxiety abated. To assist in lowering anxiety at each step of the hierarchy, she utilized relaxation and encephalic reconditioning.

Ann was also fearful of small enclosures, and she refused to use the elevator in my office building, electing to use the fire escape stairs. This elevator was used for *in vivo* exposure treatment, first with me accompanying her and later, by herself. The hierarchy was: (1) looking at people going in and out of the elevator, (2) exploring the inside of the elevator when no one was present, (3) going up one floor and exiting, and (4) re-entering the elevator and going up additional floors until the top floor was reached. When I accompanied her, I gave verbal instructions to control anxiety by encouraging her to take deep breaths and to engage in conversation. Later, several elevators in adjacent office buildings served as additional real life situations for exposure treatment.

At this point, Ann no longer had panic attacks; she was desensitized from her agoraphobia. She drove freely throughout the community and was no longer fearful of remaining home alone. She was still fearful of traveling by airplane. Exposure treatment for the phobia of flying was conducted in the same manner as for agoraphobia. Imaginal exposure using the hierarchy for fear of flying, as described in Chart 16 (page 232), was conducted. In addition, she was encouraged to go to the airport and observe passengers boarding and disembarking as well as airplanes taking off and landing. Eventually, she took a short trip with her husband and finally, longer flights. Today she flies wherever she pleases.

7. *Other Interventions* — During the course of treatment, Ann and her husband resolved marital conflicts and collaboratively addressed two of their children's academic and behavioral problems. A plan was developed for counseling and tutoring their children. Over time, the children's troublesome behavior diminished and their grades improved. As she became less symptomatic, Ann and her husband resumed social and recreational activities. The prospect of a European vacation proved to be an incentive for her to overcome her fear of flying. Elimination of stress in the marriage and family led to a happier and more satisfying life.

8. *Termination* — At the last follow up, 17 years after termination of treatment, memories of panic and agoraphobia were only dim recol-

lections in Ann's mind. Her life was stable and she was doing very well.

SUMMARY

The first step towards overcoming agoraphobia is understanding the reasons for the disorder and the methods for cure. Stopping panic attacks with antipanic medication and controlling anxiety with relaxation precedes the employment of exposure treatment. Whether conducted in imagination or in real life, exposure is the treatment of choice for overcoming the phobic restrictions of agoraphobia. During exposure treatment, it is essential that patients remain in the phobic situation until anxiety diminishes. Relaxation, thought stopping, thought substitution, and the four positive reinforcing statements help to lower anxiety. Stress from other sources must also be countered by problem-solving conferences with the spouse or family members. A resumption of social and recreational activities increases confidence and one's resolve to change. Engaging in exercise and maintaining good nutrition (see Chapter 17) also strengthens the mind and body. Overcoming agoraphobia is like having a great weight removed from the psyche. The ultimate reward is freedom to live life with peace of mind.

Part VII

Insuring Success

The Laurel Wreath and Victory

17

Finishing the Race

The treatment of panic and agoraphobia is simple, but it is not easy. Like a long-distance runner training for a race, sufferers of panic and agoraphobia must mentally and physically prepare themselves for the struggle. A commitment to examine and change lifestyles tests motivation. First, one must take stock of bad health habits. A person who abuses alcohol, poisons their body with cigarette smoke, uses illicit or non-prescribed drugs, or consumes excessive quantities of caffeine will feel jumpy, edgy, and nervous. For those who are demoralized by panic and agoraphobia and feel depressed, overwhelmed, and dispirited, can boost their morale with the knowledge that successful treatment is available.

George and Alec Gallup in their book, *The Great American Success Story*, described the results of interviews with a sample of successful people from Marquis' *Who's Who in America*. The interviewees placed a great deal of importance on old-fashioned virtues such as hard work, the desire to excel, goal-setting, and caring about people. Other success characteristics identified by the Gallups include: common sense, special knowledge, self-reliance, general intelligence, ability to get things done, inventiveness, and self-confidence. Two out of three of the productive people said that they always had pretty clear goals, both for their careers and for their lives. In almost every case, successful people set goals and formulate strategies to achieve objectives.

The results of the Gallup poll can be extrapolated to people suffering from panic and agoraphobia. Common sense, the acquisition of knowledge, and the application of information are prerequisites for overcoming panic and agoraphobia. When combined with self-confidence and persistence, the therapeutic blend leads to success. Almost all productive people set goals, develop a plan and formulate strategies to implement ideas. It seems evident, therefore, that the first step in the successful treatment of panic and agoraphobia is the development of a plan.

PLAN FOR OVERCOMING PANIC AND AGORAPHOBIA

The formula for success in overcoming panic and agoraphobia is comprised of four basic elements:

1. Goal setting
2. The development of a plan to achieve goals
3. The formulation of strategies to implement the plan
4. Perseverance

Following these four guidelines maximizes successful treatment. One may ask, "If it's that simple, why do so many people continue to suffer from panic and agoraphobia?" The truth is that there are a lot of people in the world who have overcome panic and agoraphobia. Patients who do not respond to treatment cannot, for whatever reason, follow the four simple rules.

For example, some of my colleagues tell me that they would like to write a book and ask my advice. My reply is straightforward. I relate the four principles for success. I tell them that they have already set a goal and now must develop a plan which includes researching the subject and outlining their ideas in book form. Most aspiring authors can fulfill these requirements. Next, I inform my colleagues that they must make a commitment to spend two or three hours each day working on the book until it is completed. It usually takes about a year or more to finish a book. The last requirement, "a year or more", separates authors from would-be authors. Writing, whether one feels like it or not, every day for over a year requires dedication and self-discipline. The same principle holds true for those patients who want to overcome panic and agoraphobia. The plan for conquering panic and agoraphobia is outlined below.

The program is simple, but success and the laurel wreath are awarded only to those who persevere and finish the race.

CHART 17

PLAN FOR OVERCOMING PANIC AND AGORAPHOBIA

I. Preparing the Body — Getting into Shape
   A. Establish good nutritional habits.
   B. Exercise daily.
II. Self-Education
   A. Read about panic and agoraphobia (see suggested reading list in the Appendix).
   B. Talk to recovered patients.
   C. Attend lectures on panic and agoraphobia.
   D. Join a self-help group.
   E. If unanswered questions remain, consult a professional.
III. Enhanced Communication
   A. Open up dialogue with spouse.
   B. Talk to relatives and friends.
   C. Engage in discussions with other panic-agoraphobic patients.
IV. Medication
   A. Learn about antipanic medication.
   B. Consult a physician.
   C. Take antipanic medication if prescribed.
V. Relaxation Treatment
   A. Read about the procedure.
   B. Practice the technique of relaxation daily.
   C. Utilize an audio tape to assist in practice.
   D. Employ the technique whenever needed.
VI. Encephalic Reconditioning (Changing the Videotapes of the Mind)
   A. Identify mental patterns of phobic thinking.
   B. Employ thought stopping and thought substitution.

    C. When anxiety symptoms arise, implement the four positive reinforcing statements.

    D. Practice visualizing pleasant scenes, "If everything turns out all right."

VII. Imaginal Exposure
    A. Read about the rationale and technique of desensitization.
    B. Develop a hierarchy.
    C. Carry out imaginal exposure.
    D. Employ the technique daily.

VIII. Exposure Treatment *In Vivo* (Real Life)
    A. Read about the procedure.
    B. Develop a hierarchy.
    C. Expose yourself to the lowest anxiety-evoking item on the hierarchy.
    D. Proceed to the next situation on the hierarchy when the preceding situation is mastered.
    E. Employ exposure treatment daily. At first, a spouse, friend, or therapist may assist you but eventually exposure must be done alone.
    F. Keep a diary of progress.

IX. Problem-Solving
    A. Identify significant problems.
    B. Set priorities - list the problems in order of importance.
    C. Select the most pressing problem first.
    D. Consider options and alternatives.
    E. Develop a plan which leads to a solution.
    F. Persevere.

X. Work
    A. Identify stresses at work.
    B. Develop strategies to reduce vocational stress.
    C. Discuss problems with boss.
    D. Change stressful work habits.
    E. Persevere.

XI. Social and Recreational Activities
    A. List previously enjoyed social and recreational activities.
    B. Discuss and plan pleasurable outings with spouse, relatives, and friends.

C. Engage in more social and recreational events.
D. Develop new enjoyable activities.
XII. Relapse Prevention
    A. Expect some panic-anxiety symptoms periodically.
    B. Utilize previously learned treatment techniques to cope with symptoms of panic, anxiety, and phobic behavior if they recur.
    C. Solicit understanding and support from spouse, other relatives, and friends.

I. PREPARING THE BODY — EATING AND EXERCISING

NUTRITION

We are what we eat, at least that is what an old nostrum states. One thing is for sure, what we eat or drink does affect the way we feel. If you have special dietary needs, check with your physician. The following are some nutritional rules and suggestions which will help you to prepare for successful treatment:

A. Discontinue the use of all products containing caffeine. Scientific evidence indicates that caffeine precipitates panic attacks in a majority of patients with panic disorder and also stimulates anxiety. Switch to decaffeinated coffee, herbal tea, and decaffeinated soft drinks. Look at the label of consumable products and eliminate from your diet all foodstuffs containing caffeine. Your nervous system is already hyperactive. You do not need further stimulation from products containing caffeine.

B. Stop drinking alcoholic beverages, at least temporarily. Data indicates that panic disorder is prevalent in about 20 percent of male alcoholics. My panic patients have told me that drinking even small quantities of alcohol makes them feel more prone to panic the following day. It is tempting to use alcohol to self-treat anxiety because it is widely available and lowers tension quickly. Learning to cope with panic and agoraphobia without alcohol, on the other hand, requires motivation and persistence, but it is worth the effort.

C. Don't use illicit drugs or unprescribed medications. Cocaine and "uppers" (amphetamines) stimulate the brain, which is the last thing your nervous system needs. "Downers" (barbiturates and other sedative drugs) work just like alcohol and have the same potential for abuse. Hallucinogens such as LSD can drive you crazy. Even so-called "innocuous" marijuana can send you on a bad trip, especially if it is laced with an unknown chemical. Other illicit drugs may leave you discombobulated, so that you cannot pronounce that word. If you are taking doctor-prescribed medications, check with your physician to determine if the pharmaceutical worsens panic and agoraphobia. Unless medication is required for the maintenance of health, all drugs should be discontinued.

D. Set up a well-balanced diet. A sound nutritional plan consists of adequate amounts of

257

carbohydrates, proteins, fats, and the necessary vitamins and minerals which are appropriate for your age, sex, and level of physical
activity. It is not necessary for you to go on a
"fad diet" or take huge quantities of
megavitamins. Special nutritional programs
do not cure panic and agoraphobia. But a well-
balanced diet will correct nutritional deficiencies which may interfere with treatment.

E. If you are overweight, go on a diet. You will
feel better physically and emotionally. You will
also look more attractive, thereby enhancing
your self-confidence and strengthening your
motivation.

Couch Potatoes Arise

Many people with panic and agoraphobia are
overly concerned with physical health, but do little to
improve it. Besides the improvement of the body and
mind, regular exercise desensitizes the fear associated with physical sensations. Fast heart rate, rapid
breathing, and increased muscular tension, formerly
associated with a panic attack, can now be attributed
to exercise. As desensitization occurs, panic patients
will become more tolerant of bodily sensations.
Thoughts about physical illness also diminish and
eventually disappear as the body becomes fit. Mental
fitness goes with physical fitness. Regular exercise
results in sounder sleep, more energy, mental alert-
ness, increased sex drive, less nervous tension, and a
feeling of renewal.

I am addicted to exercise. Regardless of how I feel, I either jog four or five miles or go to the gym for a workout. Afterward, I look forward to the steam room, hot tub, and a massage. I can say without reservation that following a workout I always feel better. Once you have become "hooked" on exercise, you will notice a lowering of nervous tension and an ability to cope more effectively with the nagging problems of the day.

Before starting on an exercise program, review the following suggestions:

1. You must check with your doctor and arrange for a physical examination. And if you are over 40, a stress electrocardiogram is a good idea. Once you have received a clean bill of health from your physician, the tendency to misinterpret panic-anxiety symptoms as evidence of illness will diminish. A doctor's okay to engage in regular exercise means that you are physically sound.

2. Regularity is the most important element of an exercise program. Every day you must set aside time for exercise. I schedule an hour each day for a workout, just as if I had an appointment with a patient. This time is sacrosanct and inviolable. In life, distractions and temptations abound. You must make a firm commitment to exercise daily. Nothing should supersede your appointment with yourself in the park or in a gym. Eventually, like eating, sleeping, and working, exercise will become an essential part of your life.

3. Decide upon the type of exercise that will be suitable for you. Every exercise has its advantages and disadvantages. Walking, jogging, and bicycling bring you close to nature and can be done almost anywhere. Little equipment is required, and you can exercise by yourself, or if you prefer, in the company of others. Swimming, on the other hand, requires access to a pool and during the winter, your enthusiasm may cool. Floor exercise or jazzercise groups have the advantage of meeting at regular times each week. Lifting weights can add bulk and curves to your figure; however, many solitary hours in a gym may be boring to some people and weight-lifting is essentially a non-aerobic exercise. No matter what type of exercise you choose, select one that you like and look forward to each day.

4. The goblin of procrastination can be defeated by joining a health club. Most of these organizations have a trainer who can set up a personal exercise program for you. You will be more likely to attend sessions regularly if you join a group. Later, as you begin to derive the benefits of regular exercise, self-motivation supersedes the need for supervision.

5. Don't deceive yourself. Playing golf, tennis, handball, or racquetball at irregular intervals, however laudable as recreation, cannot replace a daily 30-minute workout. It is generally acknowledged that aerobic exercises are the best for overall health. You can consult Dr.

Kenneth Cooper's books on aerobics for a full discussion of this topic.

6. *Do not expect a word of praise from your sedentary friends!* Beware of stories that loafers may tell you about the sudden death of a jogger. Look with a jaundiced eye at statements from newspapers that exercise is bad and leads to arthritis or some other malady. For laggards, the ghost of cigar smoking, brandy drinking, and obese Sir Winston Churchill is their model and patron saint. Ironically, Churchill represents an anomaly, for despite all of his bad health habits, which probably were greatly exaggerated, he lived a long and productive life. As you are preparing yourself to exercise, you may not need a doctor or a therapist, but perhaps a drill sergeant who can help you muster your resources to get yourself into shape.

SETTING THE STAGE FOR THERAPY

A commitment to change nutritional habits and engage in exercise has far reaching implications towards the successful outcome of treatment. Getting well is not a part time endeavor, but requires an overhaul of attitude and daily habits. This should not be surprising because panic and agoraphobia affect almost every aspect of daily living. A willingness to alter eating habits and improve physical fitness tests your seriousness to launch a plan which will lead to overcoming panic and agoraphobia.

II. Self Education

This book and other reading materials which are listed in the Appendix provide you with the latest information about panic and agoraphobia. Conversations with professionals may supplement this knowledge and allow you an opportunity to discuss facts which may be unclear. Talking to patients who have overcome panic and agoraphobia and sharing common experiences is also useful. Attending lectures at self-help organizations is another way of acquiring information. To puncture myths about panic and agoraphobia, it is important to get the latest data on the subject from an unimpeachable source. The power of knowledge cuts through the restraints of ignorance and hastens recovery.

III. Enhanced Communication

By now, you know as much about panic and agoraphobia as most doctors. Share this information with your family and close friends. Talk to them about your plan and enlist their help. Also, mention that their encouragement and words of praise will strengthen your resolve to get well. Enhanced communication diminishes conflict and promotes support from people who are close to you. It may be necessary to consult a therapist to assist you in clarifying details about panic and agoraphobia. Enhanced communication promotes cooperation and reduces conflicts with important people in your life.

IV. MEDICATION

If you have had several panic attacks in the last month, you must consider antipanic medication and consult a physician. The same holds true if you have disruptive panic attacks during the course of treatment. Medication not only quells panic attacks, but also calms the mind and restores control and confidence. It is disheartening when panic attacks strike during the course of treatment. Motivation may falter and some patients quit therapy.

The tricyclics, monoamine oxidase inhibitors, and benzodiazepines all block panic attacks. These three groups of antipanic medication have advantages and disadvantages which were discussed at length in Chapter 15. Any side-effects usually diminish and disappear within a few weeks. Antipanic medications are not usually associated with any serious complications. If you are healthy, take the prescribed dosage, and consult your physician at regular intervals.

V. RELAXATION TREATMENT

Learn the technique of relaxation and practice daily. After a while, you will have mastered the method and can bring forth relaxation feelings at will. Relaxation treatment instills self-control over anxiety and can be used throughout life to reduce stress and nervous tension. Instructions for progressive muscle relaxation are described in full beginning on page 210. Audio tapes facilitate the learning of relaxation and are available in most bookstores.

VI. ENCEPHALIC RECONDITIONING

CHANGING YOUR MENTAL VIDEOTAPES

The moment you make a commitment to embark upon a treatment program, your mental videotapes change from helplessness to hopefulness. Eating properly, engaging in exercise, and talking with family members about your decision to change, fosters optimism and positively affects your attitude and frame of mind. Your old habit of phobic thinking will be broken by thought stopping, thought substitution, and the four positive reinforcing statements. The negative impact of the old videotapes diminishes when you produce new ones portraying yourself coping successfully with panic and anxiety. Well-established mental habits resist change, so do not be disappointed if the old videotapes persist for a time during the first phase of treatment. Remember, your goal initially is to reduce negative thinking by 20 or 30 percent. As you improve, you will focus on the positive changes in your life. Eventually, the emotions associated with the new videotapes of the mind will predominate.

VII. IMAGINAL EXPOSURE

For those who are hesitant or fearful of engaging in real life exposure, imaginal exposure bridges the gap between the two. This process of desensitization prepares patients to confront their phobia in real life. Visualizing scenes in a hierarchial manner, as described in Chapter 16, deconditions the mind from anxiety symptoms. Imaginal exposure must be performed daily and perseverance is the key to success. Imaginal exposure requires a great deal of mental effort, but the results are worth it.

VIII. *In Vivo* Exposure Treatment

Using the hierarchy depicted on page 227 — as a guide, exposure treatment starts with the lowest anxiety-evoking item — walking from the front door of your house to the street. Stay in that situation until your anxiety diminishes and you feel reasonably calm. Proceed with the next step of the hierarchy involving a greater distance from home. You must work at exposure treatment every day, eventually completing the entire hierarchy. It is acceptable to include a spouse, friend, or therapist during the initial stages of exposure treatment. At some point, however, you must proceed unaccompanied through all steps of the hierarchy.

One exposure is not enough! You must repeatedly expose yourself to phobic situations until you feel calm and confident. As a general rule, the frequency of exposure and time spent in the phobic situation are correlated with good results. To minimize procrastination, keep a diary of your experiences and discuss your progress with a friend or therapist. Don't be discouraged if you have a brief relapse. If you stick to the program, you will be successful.

After you have completed exposure treatment involving the structured hierarchy, set up informal situations, preferably pleasurable activities that you had previously abandoned. Shopping, dining out, attending the theater, or going to a party can be addressed during unstructured exposure treatment. Remember, always stay in the situation until you feel calm and in control. Abrupt avoidance because of panic-anxiety feelings feeds the phobia and causes a setback in treatment. Exposure treatment, when diligently practiced, is extremely effective in overcoming phobic behavior.

IX. PROBLEM SOLVING

Unresolved problems cause worry, an encephalic activity which increases anxiety and interferes with treatment. The procedure for solving problems is not complicated. First, identify existing problems and arrange them in a list. Eliminate all problems which are not under your direct control and arrange the others into two categories: (1) those which require immediate attention, and (2) problems which can be deferred. Prioritize the list which requires immediate attention and work only on the first item. Consider options and alternatives as you develop a plan to solve the problem. Gather information and consult with people before you implement your solution. Solutions may not be perfect, but as problems come under some control, anxiety is lowered. After the top priority problem has been resolved to the best of your ability, go to the next item and so on, until all problems have been addressed. As is true in attaining most goals, steadfastness is the secret to successful problem-solving.

Obsessing about problems increases stress and magnifies the importance of the quandary. Don't forget, most problems in life eventually get resolved or are forgotten: "This too shall pass." Learn how to handle the little nagging problems of life. When you are being hassled, ask yourself the question, "What difference will this make tomorrow?" Often, the answer is, "Not very much." Dispel those small nagging problems from your mind. Spend your energy only on realistic problems which have an important bearing on your life.

X. WORK

Salaried or unsalaried work is often a source of stress. As in problem-solving, work stress must be identified and strategies developed to combat it. Discussions with fellow employees and a conference with the boss can illuminate factors contributing to job stress. Develop a plan to reduce conflicts at work and to make work easier and less stressful for you. Most employers are aware of the relationship between happy workers and productivity. If it can be demonstrated that stressful work habits interfere with job performance, most employers will approve of change.

Job performance may be directly affected by panic and agoraphobia. Panic attacks, phobic avoidance, and phobic thinking disrupt concentration and interfere with most occupations. One of the benefits of successful treatment is improved occupational performance and greater personal satisfaction. Common sense and perseverance help to resolve conflicts at work and to reduce anxiety symptoms. Dogged determination helps to resolve conflicts at work and to reduce anxiety symptoms.

XI. Social/Recreational Activities

At first glance, it may seem that socializing with people and having fun is natural and spontaneous. However, we have all experienced lonely weekends because of a failure to plan social and recreational activities. In panic and agoraphobia, fear blocks avenues of enjoyment. Once panic and agoraphobia have been conquered, the pursuit of pleasure is one of the rewards for getting well. The desire for social and recreational outings must be communicated to your spouse, relatives, or friends. Forgotten fun can be resurrected and new pastimes planned. Instead of presaging panic and anxiety, you can presage pleasure as you look forward to entertaining encounters. Trips to places previously avoided can add adventure, excitement, and fulfillment to life.

XII. Relapse Prevention

After treatment has been terminated, the biggest fear of many patients is suffering a relapse. It is realistic to expect some symptoms following termination but not a complete collapse. Rather than worry, it is more fruitful to remember the treatment methods which proved to be effective. Cure is not a house of cards, and the sudden eruption of symptoms will not result in a toppling of the entire structure of recovery. More often than not, if panic attacks recur, the symptoms will diminish without extensive intervention. It may only be necessary to "ride out" a panic attack by employing relaxation treatment and encephalic interventions. If phobic symptoms or, more likely, phobic thinking reappear, it is usually for a short period of time. If symptoms reappear, it is important to keep calm, reinstitute treatment methods, remain optimistic, and seek support from your family. And, if needed, consult a therapist. Don't panic! A relapse should be considered only as an annoyance which requires intervention.

SUCCESSFUL TREATMENT

Treatment is deemed successful when: (1) panic attacks cease, (2) phobic avoidance is no longer a problem, and (3) patients resume normal activities unrestricted by panic or agoraphobia. Whether medication should be continued depends upon each patient's response to slow withdrawal. If panic attacks and phobic avoidance do not return, antipanic medication can be terminated. For many patients, especially those who have changed their lifestyle, medication is no longer necessary.

Sisyphus or Success?

18

Success or Failure

Sisyphus, the legendary king of Corinth, was condemned to a life spent rolling a heavy stone up a steep mountain in Hades, only to have it roll down again as it neared the top. Whether a panic and agoraphobic sufferer chooses the Sisyphian solution of lifelong failure or elects to climb the mountain in triumphant success depends upon the qualities of perseverance and determination. The medical and psychological treatment for overcoming panic and agoraphobia are available, yet some afflicted people continue to pay penance to Pan and retreat into the syndrome of agoraphobia.

Each week patients come to my office complaining that treatment by other doctors has not been successful. The patients are suffering. They seem sincere. And they desperately want help. I ask myself, "Why has previous medical and psychological treatment failed?" My inquiries have led me to compile a list of reasons why treatment is not always successful.

REASONS FOR TREATMENT FAILURES

1. The wrong diagnosis was made.
2. Treatment recommendations were not followed.
3. Patients maintained an unshakable belief that their symptoms were due to a physical illness.
4. Panic attacks continued despite medication ("symptom breakthrough").
5. The patient refused antipanic medication.
6. Exposure treatment was improperly conducted.
7. The spouse and family members were not involved in treatment.
8. The patient had a "flight into health", although nothing had really changed.
9. The patient feared or distrusted doctors.
10. The patient abused alcohol or other drugs.
11. A severe depression interfered with treatment.
12. The patient precipitously quit treatment.
13. There was unremitting stress from problems not associated with panic or agoraphobia.
14. The patient relapsed due to one or more of the above.

WRONG DIAGNOSIS

A wrong diagnosis delays proper treatment. Although panic and agoraphobia have received widespread coverage in scientific journals as well as in the public media, some professionals are unaware of the typical signs, symptoms, and clinical course of this disorder. Many times I have seen panic-agoraphobic patients misdiagnosed as having another mental disorder. Although not common, some physical disorders may mimic panic and agoraphobia. To ensure that a correct diagnosis will be made, one must first consult a physician for a complete physical examination. Next, seek the opinion of an anxiety expert, preferably a psychiatrist, psychologist, or social worker associated with an anxiety and phobia clinic or a university. Panic and agoraphobia have specific, easily identifiable symptoms and a predictable clinical course which is not ambiguous. A properly conducted examination should lead to the correct diagnosis.

NONCOMPLIANCE WITH TREATMENT RECOMMENDATIONS

During lectures to medical and social work students, I often state that if my patients followed my instructions, they would all get well. However, not all of my patients follow my advice or prescriptions for cure. I have come to the ironic conclusion that some of my patients would rather talk than change. Dr. Isaac M. Marks, an acknowledged expert on anxiety disorders, has observed that treatment occurs within a "dual process framework" involving motivation and execution. The patient must carry out specific tasks in order to bring about a resolution of the presenting problem.

Procrastination is a nemesis common to all of us. People resist change because it is anxiety-evoking. This is doubly true of some patients with panic and agoraphobia. A suggestion to embark upon an exposure treatment program which is temporarily anxiety-evoking can be misinterpreted. The patient may think that the therapist doesn't understand or is heartless. Agoraphobics may mistakenly believe that exposure treatment will place them in great danger. The anxiety associated with actual exposure to phobic situations, e.g., going greater distances from home unaccompanied, is always less than one would imagine. The same is true of panic attacks. Although one may have an occasional panic attack during the course of treatment, the experience is rarely overwhelming. Panic and anxiety are controllable, especially when coping techniques that have been described in this book are utilized.

Sometimes noncompliance results from lack of information. Patients may terminate therapy because they do not understand instructions and the rationale for treatment. Self-education — reading articles or books, talking with other panic-agoraphobic patients, or consulting a knowledgeable professional — helps to defeat this reason for failure.

Drs. C. Barr Taylor and Bruce Arno in a recent book, *The Nature and Treatment of Anxiety Disorders*, agree that insufficient information regarding the benefits of performing prescribed tasks is a frequent problem in therapy. They also mention that non-compliance is sometimes due to low self-efficacy. Putting it another way, there's a low estimation on the patient's part that he or she can successfully carry out therapeutic tasks.

Another reason for noncompliance is a perceived high cost/benefit ratio in which the benefits are believed insufficient for the patient to tolerate the temporary discomfort involved in treatment. Taylor and Arno also point to secondary gain issues perceived to reduce the benefits of improvement. Secondary gain refers to cases in which the patient's symptoms provide some significant benefit which overrides cure. Indeed, some dispirited patients lose confidence in themselves and become overly dependent on a spouse, friend, or even a therapist. For those who conclude that a high cost/benefit and secondary gain are volitional choices, a reappraisal is in order. Symptomatic behavior prompted by fear is never personally advantageous. The freedom to choose where we go, with whom we associate, and what we think is at risk in patients with panic and agoraphobia. I have always felt uncomfortable about concepts concerning cost/benefit and secondary gain because they imply that the patient wants to remain sick. A better explanation is that patients do not know a way out of their quandary and require direction and support. Appropriate treatment can reverse self-defeating behavior related to issues of high cost/benefit ratio and secondary gain.

BELIEF IN PHYSICAL ILLNESS

At the beginning of treatment, victims of panic are extremely vulnerable and often ascribe symptoms to a physical illness. Continuing symptoms fuel the falsehood of physical disease and clinging to this notion interferes with treatment. To counter any doubt about the diagnosis of panic disorder, the results of physical examinations and laboratory tests should be reviewed. Patients ought to understand that existing symptoms are anxiety-based and do not reflect a medical disease. When symptoms diminish in intensity or disappear, the incorrect belief in physical illness also vanishes.

PANIC ATTACKS PERSIST DESPITE MEDICATION

When panic attacks continue during treatment, it is an ominous sign that means: (1) the prescribed dosage of antipanic medication is too low, (2) there has been a "symptom break-through" indicating that the current dosage of medication is now insufficient, (3) the patient is not taking the antipanic medication as prescribed, or (4) the patient misinterprets surges of anxiety as evidence of a panic attack.

Once a therapeutic level of antipanic medication has been reached, panic attacks almost always cease. At the beginning of treatment, before the proper dosage of antipanic medication has been attained, panic attacks may occur sporadically. As the dose of medicine is increased, patients must be patient and learn to cope with the temporary panic sensations.

Some patients who have been on medication for several months without any panic attacks experience a "symptom break-through". No one knows why this happens; however, the solution is simple — raise the dose of antipanic medication. Once the dose of medication has been adjusted, panic attacks again are brought under control.

A few patients accept a prescription for medication, but fail to have it filled. Still others who are timid and fearful of side-effects may take medication in doses lower than prescribed. Patients must be honest about consumption of the prescribed medication and accurately report the dose to their doctor. To determine the dose of medication in the body with accuracy, some physicians obtain a blood test.

REFUSAL TO TAKE MEDICATION

Some patients who have frequent panic attacks may refuse to take medication. They are frightened and feel that a pharmaceutical agent will precipitate a panic attack or be harmful in some way. This irrational fear or phobia of taking medicine can be overcome by persuasion and desensitization. Beginning with very low doses of antipanic medication, side-effects will be minimal or nonexistent. As the dose is slowly increased, patients will gradually become accustomed to taking medication without fear. Once the benefit of desensitization occurs and the medication takes effect, the phobia becomes insignificant.

Occasionally, a patient rejects biological treatment (medication) in favor of solely a psychological approach. This may indicate an underlying phobia of taking medicine or an honest desire to be drug free. If panic attacks are infrequent, it may not be unreasonable to proceed without medication, provided the attacks do not interfere with psychological treatment.

EXPOSURE TREATMENT
"DOESN'T WORK"

The dropout rate associated with exposure treatment has been estimated to be approximately 12 percent. Some patients simply cannot or will not tolerate the discomfort associated with exposure. Proceeding too rapidly is a common mistake. Jumping ahead to a more anxiety-evoking item on the hierarchy before a lower step has been mastered can lead to a panic attack or high anxiety. In turn, this can result in the incorrect conclusion that exposure "doesn't work". Graduated exposure, on the other hand, is structured to prevent patients from experiencing high levels of anxiety. By selecting the lowest anxiety-evoking item on the hierarchy and utilizing relaxation and other coping techniques, anxiety is manageable.

A study by Dr. Andrew M. Mathews and his colleagues disclosed that therapist assisted exposure is one possible explanation for failure. Once the therapist is withdrawn, the potential for relapse is higher. Relapses are less common when exposure is spouse assisted or conducted in a group. To assure total recovery, exposure treatment can be conducted in a variety of circumstances; however, eventually, it must be self-directed. If properly conducted, exposure is the most effective treatment for agoraphobia.

SPOUSE OR FAMILY MEMBERS
NOT INVOLVED

The spouse or other family members can inadvertently sabotage treatment. By complying with irrational
requests of the patient, phobic or dependent behavior is reinforced. This obstruction can be removed if
the spouse participates in enhanced communication
sessions and learn about panic and agoraphobia. Dr.
David H. Barlow and his colleagues compared treatment with two agoraphobic groups: one in which
husbands attended all sessions and participated fully
in treatment, and another in which husbands were
thanked for their willingness to participate, but were
told it was not necessary. Barlow's findings indicated
that including the husbands in the treatment process
produced substantial clinical advantages with 12 out
of 14 clients. The spouse assisted group also showed
gains in social, work, and family functioning. Patients
in the non-spouse treatment group did not do as well
and took longer to achieve benefits in social and
occupational functioning.

An unhealthy codependency between a patient
and spouse always obstructs treatment. The unaf-
fected spouse may prefer, either consciously or un-
consciously, to maintain a relationship in which the
other member remains sick. Consider the consequences of cure for one husband who told me that if
his wife ever overcame agoraphobia, she would leave
him. In this case, marital therapy with a professional
was indicated to unravel the unhealthy co-dependency
relationship. During therapy, most couples discover

that marriages flourish in an atmosphere of shared benevolence. When marital conflicts cannot be worked out, protracted unhappiness and slow or no response to treatment is the patient's lot. Divorce is sometimes a solution sought by a disaffected spouse.

FLIGHT INTO HEALTH

Sometimes patients report a "flight into health" after only a few sessions of treatment. I am usually stunned by this sudden declaration of independence, but my surprise evaporates after an analysis of the case. An unexpected termination of treatment usually means that the panic-agoraphobic patient has reservations about making a commitment to change. Fear forms the basis of this resistance to alter behavior. The patient prefers to adapt to the limitations imposed by panic and agoraphobia instead of undertaking a program of treatment. A meeting, preferably involving the patient, spouse, and a professional, can help to reduce fear associated with change. Positive expectations and benefits which go along with improvement can be contrasted with the detrimental effects of negative, self-defeating behavior. One tactic that I have found useful is to bring together a recovered patient with a reluctant one. The patient who has overcome panic and agoraphobia often motivates new patients to continue with therapy. Enrollment in a panic and agoraphobic self-help group is another option. Ultimately, after all the information has been presented, the patient must decide.

FEAR OR DISTRUST OF DOCTORS

Most people feel apprehensive about seeing a doctor. In agoraphobia, however, the central fear of leaving home includes going to a doctor's office. To reduce fear, many patients come to their first office visit accompanied by family members. In some cases, I make a home visit to attend those patients who are housebound. When patients have been placed on medication and have learned relaxation, the phobia of going to a doctor's office usually diminishes. After exposure treatment has been successfully concluded, the fear disappears.

If previous treatment has failed, some patients blame the doctor and develop a distrust of all therapists. Rather than disparage doctors and shy away from treatment, it is more fruitful to consult a clinician who specializes in anxiety and phobic disorders. During sessions of education and enhanced communication, previous therapy can be analyzed and reasons for failure discussed. New goals should be defined, and patients need to understand the rationale underlying treatment methods and to agree to follow instructions. Treatment seldom goes smoothly, especially at the beginning. Difficulties which arise in treatment can be ironed out through discussion between the patient and doctor.

ABUSE OF ALCOHOL OR OTHER DRUGS

Alcohol and drug abuse complicate the treatment of panic and agoraphobia. If abuse or dependency problems exist, they must be addressed along with treatment for panic-agoraphobia. For those who have become dependent upon alcohol or other drugs, the goal of treatment is abstinence. Because of the mental mechanism of denial which is common to most substance abusers, the extent of addiction may not be acknowledged. A conference with a family member should always involve questions concerning patterns of alcohol and drug abuse. The coexistence of panic-agoraphobia and psychoactive substance use disorder makes for a poor prognosis unless the patient submits to treatment and gives up his addiction.

SEVERE DEPRESSION

There is a relationship between depression and anxiety, but these are two distinct mental disorders which require two modes of treatment. The sad, blue, and down in the dumps feeling of depression is associated with pessimism, sleep problems, appetite disturbance, suicidal thoughts, feelings of guilt, hopelessness, and a general inability to cope with life or experience pleasure. Depression saps energy and destroys motivation. In a quagmire of indecision and self-pity, it is difficult for depressed patients to implement a treatment program for panic and agoraphobia. The solution is straight-forward — treat the depression. Happily, most of the symptoms of depression can be reversed with the use of antidepressant medication and psychotherapy. In most cases, when depression is alleviated, treatment for panic and agoraphobia proceeds more smoothly. Also, reduction of panic and phobic symptoms is uplifting and helps to allay depression.

THE PATIENT QUITS PRECIPITOUSLY

When a patient drops out of treatment suddenly and without explanation, the cause may never be discovered. Any of the foregoing reasons for failure could be responsible, but one really never knows. When patients drop out of treatment without notification, it is very distressing to me. The patient will continue to suffer and I will never have the opportunity to treat them. I do attempt to contact patients who precipitously stop therapy, but I seldom receive a rational reason for termination. Sometimes, dropouts will say that they do not have the time or money to continue treatment. Still others insist that their panic and agoraphobia are not very serious. Occasionally, I can persuade a patient to return, but more often dropouts refuse to discuss options for continuing therapy. For the patient, a decision to quit treatment means ongoing disability. This sad state is particularly unfortunate because effective treatment is available.

RELAPSES

Much the same as with other illnesses, patients with panic and agoraphobia may regress following improvement. Life is never anxiety-free and mild or moderate anxiety may be misinterpreted as a full-blown panic attack. Everyone is exposed to stressful situations and must deal with disappointments, disagreeable people, tragedy, and the problems of daily living. The best advice for panic patients is: Don't panic! Instead, using the concept of the Three E's, figure out the source of anxiety and employ therapeutic techniques. Learning how to cope with everyday stress has prophylactic value and allows patients to assume control over their lives.

After panic attacks have ceased and phobic behavior is no longer troublesome, phobic thinking still remains for a while. To avoid slipping back into old thinking habits which increase anxiety, encephalic interventions should be continued and combined with problem solving. As things return to normal, thinking will begin to reflect the improvement in one's life.

The belief that once cured, panic and agoraphobic symptoms will never return is perhaps the greatest danger regarding retrogression. If some symptoms return, disillusion may lead to disparaging previous treatment. Enhanced communication, medication, relaxation, exposure treatment, and other antianxiety interventions need only be applied again to achieve control of symptoms.

Dr. L. Jansson and his colleagues proposed a rigorous maintenance or relapse prevention program for agoraphobics. His program included a commitment from the patient's spouse or significant other to ensure that *in vivo* exposure will continue after termination. High risk situations which might cause setbacks were identified and strategies for dealing with these were planned. Each patient was required to submit a monthly report dealing with progress.

The results from this research indicated that gains from initial treatment had been maintained during the follow-up period.

When I mention termination of treatment to my panic-agoraphobic patients, they become apprehensive and inwardly fear a relapse. Later, if symptoms return, I have discovered that patients may be hesitant to call for an appointment because they feel embarrassed and blame themselves. The reluctance to make another appointment is often based on the feeling that they are incurable or have let me down. For these reasons, I insist that my patients return for periodic follow-ups after termination. Consultations are available whenever needed without fostering an unhealthy dependency. Routinely, I schedule follow-ups at three month intervals during the first year. I tell my patients that illness comes and goes throughout life, and panic and agoraphobia are no exception. If symptoms of panic-agoraphobia recur, they can be reversed by using the same methods which worked previously.

SUCCESS

From a psychiatrist's standpoint, one of the positive things about panic and agoraphobia is that it is amenable to successful treatment. The preceding reasons for failure do not occur frequently. Over the course of twenty-five years of clinical practice, I have seen patients cope successfully with all of the above reasons associated with failure. Sufferers can overcome panic and agoraphobia by themselves, or if medication is needed, by consulting a psychiatrist. Long, drawn-out treatment is unnecessary. Tenacity and a commitment to change are fundamental requirements for success.

The ultimate reward for overcoming panic and agoraphobia is freedom: freedom to do anything and go where you please, freedom from the belief that you have something physically wrong with you, and freedom from thoughts that you must avoid certain situations or have someone accompany you at all times. Recovery is complete when you are able to work and love as you choose. One thing is certain, the enjoyment of life is anathema to panic and agoraphobia. As the world becomes a source of satisfaction and pleasure, Pan retreats farther into the dark forest as you pass from panic to peace of mind.

Appendix I

PANIC CHECKLIST

The panic checklist has been designed to help you identify and categorize panic symptoms. It is meant to be a guide, not a diagnostic instrument. Once oriented to the concept of panic disorder, recognition of symptoms requires no professional degree. Common sense and correct identification of symptoms, along with information concerning the clinical course of the disorder, leads to the diagnosis. After reading the items on the panic checklist, mark the appropriate answer, yes or no, before each statement.

Yes   No

☐   ☐   1. Were you between the ages of 18 and 35 when you had your first panic attack?

☐   ☐   2. Following a physical examination, did your doctor tell you that there was nothing seriously wrong with you or that you were just suffering from "a case of nerves"?

☐   ☐   3. Was the attack associated with the worst emotional feeling that you have ever experienced?

☐   ☐   4. Despite normal physical examinations, did you think that there was still something physically wrong with you?

☐   ☐   5. After being told you had nothing physically wrong with you, did these attacks continue?

☐   ☐   6. Do you often think about having another attack?

☐   ☐   7. Do these attacks interfere significantly with your life (restrict your activities or prevent you from going certain places)?

If you answered yes to each of the preceding questions, the chances are very high that you have panic disorder. Discuss this matter with a professional who has expertise in the area of anxiety disorders. Although medical conditions can mimic some signs and symptoms of panic disorder, they are few in number and can be easily ruled out by your physician.

Appendix II

THE PANIC PROFILE

ENCEPHALIC ACTIVITIES

Encephalic activity refers to thoughts, fantasies and visual images which evoke fear or anxiety. In the following list, please check the box which most frequently indicates the *time* you spend thinking about the following subjects. If you check the box marked one (1), that subject is not on your mind at all. If you check the box marked five (5), this means that topic is on your mind almost constantly. Boxes two (2), three (3), and four (4) indicate intermediate degrees of time you may spend thinking about these subjects.

	1 Not at All	2 A Little	3 A Fair Amount	4 Much	5 Very Much
1. Dying	☐	☐	☐	☐	☐
2. Disease or illness	☐	☐	☐	☐	☐
3. Insanity (going crazy)	☐	☐	☐	☐	☐
4. Being out of control	☐	☐	☐	☐	☐
5. Panic	☐	☐	☐	☐	☐
6. Being trapped	☐	☐	☐	☐	☐
7. Embarrassment or humiliation	☐	☐	☐	☐	☐
8. Rejection or disapproval	☐	☐	☐	☐	☐
9. Impending doom	☐	☐	☐	☐	☐
10. Fainting	☐	☐	☐	☐	☐

ENDOGENOUS SENSATIONS

Endogenous sensations refer to the physiological (physical) sensations within your body. In panic disorder, the symptoms represent anxiety and are *not* due to any illness or disease process. The physiologic sensations may be entirely normal, such as when a person notices rapid breathing or his heart beating fast following vigorous activity such as exercise. In the list below, check the appropriate box which indicates the *frequency* that you have experienced the following symptoms. If you check one (1), it indicates that you have not experienced this symptom at all. If you check five (5), it indicates that you experience that symptom almost all of the time. Boxes two (2), three (3), and four (4) indicate intermediate frequency.

	1 Not at All	2 A Little	3 A Fair Amount	4 Much	5 Very Much
1. Smothering	☐	☐	☐	☐	☐
2. Choking	☐	☐	☐	☐	☐
3. Nausea	☐	☐	☐	☐	☐
4. Vomiting	☐	☐	☐	☐	☐
5. Heart beating fast	☐	☐	☐	☐	☐
6. Tightness of the chest	☐	☐	☐	☐	☐
7. Dizziness	☐	☐	☐	☐	☐
8. Tingly feelings in the arms or legs (especially the hands)	☐	☐	☐	☐	☐
9. Feeling faint	☐	☐	☐	☐	☐
10. Trembling	☐	☐	☐	☐	☐
11. Blurry vision	☐	☐	☐	☐	☐
12. Feeling unreal (or like another person)	☐	☐	☐	☐	☐

Scoring the Panic Profile

All items that have been checked five (5) are worth five points, four (4) are worth four points, and so forth. If you score between 88 and 110 points, you definitely have panic disorder. If you score between 65 and 87, there is a strong possibility that you do have panic disorder. If you score between 44 and 65, you may be suffering from chronic anxiety unless you have had a panic attack in the last month, in which case you are suffering from panic disorder. Scores under 44 are within the normal range. These results should be checked with your doctor or therapist. Only a physical and mental status examination can definitely diagnose panic disorder.

Appendix III

AGORAPHOBIA CHECKLIST

The recognition of agoraphobia may be easy or difficult, depending upon the severity of the phobia. To help determine whether you have agoraphobia, the following Agoraphobia Checklist has been devised. As you consider each item, check the degree of anxiety which applies at the time you fill out the checklist. How you felt last week or last year does not indicate your current functioning.

Check the appropriate box which indicates the degree of anxiety or fear (nervousness) that each item would cause you at the present time.

	1 Not at All	2 A Little	3 A Fair Amount	4 Much	5 Very Much
1. Being alone	☐	☐	☐	☐	☐
2. Crossing streets	☐	☐	☐	☐	☐
3. Going to a dentist, barber, beauty shop	☐	☐	☐	☐	☐
4. Driving a car	☐	☐	☐	☐	☐
5. Riding in a car	☐	☐	☐	☐	☐
6. Riding in a train	☐	☐	☐	☐	☐
7. Journeys by plane	☐	☐	☐	☐	☐
8. Riding in a bus	☐	☐	☐	☐	☐
9. Travel by boat	☐	☐	☐	☐	☐
10. Crowds	☐	☐	☐	☐	☐
11. Being in an elevator	☐	☐	☐	☐	☐
12. Parting from friends	☐	☐	☐	☐	☐
13. Enclosed places	☐	☐	☐	☐	☐
14. Doctors	☐	☐	☐	☐	☐
15. Large, open spaces	☐	☐	☐	☐	☐
16. Leaving home	☐	☐	☐	☐	☐
17. Bridges	☐	☐	☐	☐	☐
18. Heavy traffic	☐	☐	☐	☐	☐
19. Expressways	☐	☐	☐	☐	☐
20. Being in public places	☐	☐	☐	☐	☐
21. Attending meetings	☐	☐	☐	☐	☐
22. Waiting in lines	☐	☐	☐	☐	☐
23. Eating in restaurants	☐	☐	☐	☐	☐
24. Exercise	☐	☐	☐	☐	☐
25. Speaking in front of a group	☐	☐	☐	☐	☐
26. Going to visit a friend's house alone	☐	☐	☐	☐	☐
27. Leaving home for at least 15 minutes	☐	☐	☐	☐	☐
28. Traveling through a tunnel alone	☐	☐	☐	☐	☐
29. Being in a new place	☐	☐	☐	☐	☐
30. Escalators	☐	☐	☐	☐	☐
31. Going into a church or theater	☐	☐	☐	☐	☐
32. Going to work each day	☐	☐	☐	☐	☐

SCORING THE AGORAPHOBIC CHECKLIST

All items that have been checked five (5) are worth 5 points, four (4) are worth 4 points, and so forth. If you scored between 128 and 160, you definitely have agoraphobia. If you scored between 95 and 127, there is a strong possibility that you do have agoraphobia. If you scored between 64 and 95, you may be suffering from a phobia, though not necessarily agoraphobia. Scores under 64 are usually not significant. Remember, only a physical and mental status examination can definitely diagnose agoraphobia.

Appendix IV

SUGGESTED READINGS

Agras, W. S. *Panic: Facing Fears, Phobias, and Anxiety.* New York: W. H. Freeman, 1985.

Barlow, D. H. and Cerny, J. A. *Psychological Treatment of Panic.* New York: The Guilford Press, 1988.

Cooper, K. H. *The Aerobic Way.* New York: M. Evans & Co., 1977.

Davis, M., Eshelman, E. R., and McKay, M. *The Relaxation and Stress Reduction Workbook 2nd Ed.* Oakland: New Harbinger Publication, 1982.

Dupont. R. L., (Ed.) *Phobia: A Comprehensive Summary of Modern Treatment.* New York: Brunner/ Mazel, Inc., 1982.

Eischens, R. R. and Greist, J. H. *Running Guides.*

Madison: Anxiety Disorder Center, 1980.

Goldstein, A. and Stainback, B. *Overcoming Agoraphobia: Conquering Fear of the Outside World.* New York: Viking, 1987.

Goodwin, D. W. *Anxiety.* New York: Oxford University Press, 1986.

Greist, J. H., Jefferson, J. W., and Marks, I. M. *Anxiety and Its Treatment.* New York: Warner Books, 1986.

Matthews, A. M., Gelder, M. G., and Johnston, D. W. *Agoraphobia: Nature and Treatment.* New York: The Guilford Press, 1981.

Scrignar, C. B. *Stress Strategies: The Treatment of the Anxiety Disorders.* Basel: Karger, 1983.

Scrignar, C. B. *Post-Traumatic Stress Disorder: Diagnosis, Treatment, and Legal Issues, 2nd Ed.* New Orleans: Bruno Press, 1988.

Sheehan, D. V. *The Anxiety Disease.* New York: Bantam Books, 1983.

Wolpe, J. *The Practice of Behavior Therapy, 3rd Ed.* New York: Pergamon Press, 1982.

FOR READERS DESIRING MORE DETAIL, THE FOLLOWING BOOKS ARE RECOMMENDED

Ballenger, J. C. (Ed.) *Biology of Agoraphobia.* Washington, D. C.: American Psychiatric Press, Inc., 1984.

Beck, A. T. and Emery, G. *Anxiety Disorders and Phobias: A Cognitive Perspective.* New York: Basic Books, 1985.

Last, C. G. and Hersen, M., (Eds.) *Handbook of Anxiety Disorders.* New York: Pergamon Press, 1988.

Marks, I. M. *Fears, Phobias, and Rituals: Panic, Anxiety and Their Disorders.* New York: Oxford University Press, 1987.

Mavissakalian, M. and Barlow, D. *Phobia: Psychological and Pharmacological Treatment.* New York: The Guilford Press, 1981.

Taylor, C. B. and Arnow, B. *The Nature and Treatment of Anxiety Disorders.* New York: The Free Press, 1988.

SELF-HELP ORGANIZATIONS

TERRAP (Territorial Apprehensiveness)
Arthur B. Hardy, M.D.
1010 Doyle Street, Suite 8
Menlo Park, California   94025
415-321-0300

The Anxiety Disorders Association of America
6000 Executive Boulevard, Suite 200
Rockville, Maryland   20852–3801
301-231-9350

Index

About the Author

C. B. Scrignar, M.S., M.D., received his training in medicine and psychiatry at Tulane University School of Medicine in New Orleans. Dr. Scrignar studied behavior therapy at Temple University under the guidance of Dr. Joseph Wolpe. This experience stimulated his interest in behavior therapy and he began teaching courses on the subject at Tulane University School of Medicine and School of Social Work. He has written extensively about behavior therapy, forensic psychiatry, stress and anxiety disorders, drug addiction, human sexuality, crime and delinquency, and hypnosis. He has also written two other books: *Stress Strategies: The Treatment of the Anxiety Disorders* and *Post-Traumatic Stress Disorder: Diagnosis, Treatment and Legal Issues.* Currently, Dr. Scrignar is in the private practice of psychiatry and is a clinical professor of psychiatry at Tulane University School of Medicine and an adjunct professor of social work at Tulane University School of Social Work.